F

-8

D1595776

CROSSING BACK

Crossing Back

BOOKS, FAMILY, AND MEMORY WITHOUT PAIN

Marianna De Marco Torgovnick

FORDHAM UNIVERSITY PRESS   NEW YORK   2021

Frontispiece: Modica, Sicily. Photo by Barry Hoffman.

Fordham University Press has no responsibility for the persistence or accuracy of URLs for external or third-party Internet websites referred to in this publication and does not guarantee that any content on such websites is, or will remain, accurate or appropriate.

Fordham University Press also publishes its books in a variety of electronic formats. Some content that appears in print may not be available in electronic books.

Visit us online at www.fordhampress.com.

Library of Congress Cataloging-in-Publication Data

Names: Torgovnick, Marianna, (date) author.
Title: Crossing back : books, family, and memory without pain / Marianna De Marco Torgovnick.
Description: First edition. | New York : Fordham University Press, 2021. | Includes bibliographical references and index.
Identifiers: LCCN 2021027352 | ISBN 9780823297788 (hardback) | ISBN 9780823297795 (epub)
Subjects: LCSH: Torgovnick, Marianna, (date) author. | Authors, American — 21st century — Biography. | Italian American women — Biography. | Grief — Biography. | Books and reading — Psychological aspects.
Classification: LCC PS3620.O587488 Z46 2021 | DDC 814/.6 [B] — dc23
LC record available at https://lccn.loc.gov/2021027352

Printed in the United States of America

23 22 21   5 4 3 2 1

First edition

To Rosie and Parker

Contents

Prologue

When you complete a book and send it into the world, there are always events that might surprise or even overwhelm it. *Crossing Back* encountered just such events when COVID-19 shut things down, changing what we used to consider life as normal, making the very word "normal" enough to bring us to tears. In the midst of mourning for 581,056 dead Americans and counting,[1] the ethics of writing about two personal losses made me confront once again a question addressed in the book: How does one claim personal grief about a mother's death, a brother's, amid national crisis and worldwide pain? As Edwidge Danticat says in a recent essay about an elderly neighbor's death, "It's hard to figure out how to mourn during a pandemic."[2] And yet, having written about her own mother's death from ovarian cancer and mentioning it in her essay, Danticat also knows that it's hard in general to figure out how to mourn a mother's death, a brother's. Such loss continues to cut deep, even amid larger tragedies.

One hundred thousand Americans dead from COVID-19 in mid-May, 2020, two hundred thousand on September 22, and over three hundred thousand by the end of that year.[3] Over five hundred thousand as I write and more certain by the time *Crossing Back* appears. Surge upon surge, sometimes in exponential growth. A huge loss. A national mourning. The numbers can stagger or even paralyze the mind, and they become most real to us when they connect to individuals and to personal histories. For we process loss not just in the aggregate but in the particulars. That was true after 1945 in accounts of the atomic bombing at Hiroshima. It was true after 9/11 in memorials to the dead. It remains true in narratives of the Holocaust up to today.[4] As the acerbic critic Georges Bataille noted in "Concerning the Accounts Given by the Residents of Hiroshima," an essay published in 1947: "Let's admit it. The population of hell increases annually by fifty million souls. A world war [an atomic bombing, a pandemic] may accelerate the rhythm slightly, but it cannot significantly alter it." That's true. Yet Bataille was moved to write by the personal testimonies gathered by John Hersey in his famous 1946 book.[5]

For much of the pandemic, and documented by the fall of 2020, it was abundantly clear that in the U.S. the brunt of the pandemic has been borne by Black and Latinx groups, a higher percentage of whom did not have the luxury of working from home: For Blacks and Latinx, some figures cited were 18 percent and 17 percent versus 30 percent for Whites.[6] Such ratios continued through the pandemic: By December 2020, statistics showed that people of color and Indigenous groups had three times the number of cases and were five times more likely to die.[7] With equal starkness, mortality figures showed the danger of preexisting conditions, once again found in higher proportions among Blacks, Latinx, and the Indigenous. In that context, people who refused to stay at home as much as possible during surges or to wear masks in public asserted not just their right to "freedom," as they claimed, but also White privilege. The same fact cuts the other way too: Those able to stay home depended on new categories of "essential workers" who shopped and delivered groceries and other supplies.

The COVID-19 pandemic was always going to be bad, but it did not have to be as bad as it has been in the United States, with (as I write) the highest death toll worldwide, many schools and businesses closed, people separated long-term from families, and a volatile and fractious nation. By mid-September 2020, the deaths from COVID-19 equaled, *every three days*, those on 9/11, which triggered national trauma and the invasion of Iraq; by December 2020, that number of deaths happened every day and continued for months. The total number of American deaths from the pandemic now exceeds combat deaths in World War I, World War II, and Vietnam, combined: one more shocking landmark.[8] There's talk again of matching the 675,000 Americans lost in the 1918 pandemic, which once seemed unthinkable. We have vaccines—a ray of hope—and people are getting them, changing things rapidly. But what the precise situation will be by the end of the pandemic, it's impossible to say.

Memory works in strange ways for individuals and for groups, with devious paths that range from indelible events that define generations—the Great Depression, World War II—through identification and empathy, all the way to denial and repression. How will we remember the seasons of COVID-19?[9] The trauma of 2020? The Trump presidency, the election of 2020, and the change that Biden makes? The wave of sentiment for racial justice that has galvanized the young and swept the nation? Will they mostly be erased from cultural memory, like the anthrax scare that followed 9/11? Remembered selectively and differently, perhaps along political lines? Or, as one suspects, and despite the strong urge for a return to normalcy, will they be remembered for decades to come, the pandemic and lockdown having lasted too long, cut too deep, and hit too close to home to be forgotten, its having made heaven knows what impression on young minds separated for months, and even years, from family and friends?

Like many of us, I have felt perfectly dreadful many times during the COVID-19 crisis. I remember the imprint of my granddaughters' warm bodies against my own and miss that once-regular sensation. I spend afternoons with my Duke classes on Zoom, trying to hear my students' pain and to ease it. I remember the day George Floyd died, the one when Jacob Blake was riddled with bullets in front of his three young sons. The day I heard that Danny's stepfather, my friend Becky's father-in-law, died of the virus in Queens, New York, and that his mother was ill but recovering into a changed future. Though Becky is originally my daughter's friend, she thoughtfully delivered to my front door the makings of ice cream sundaes on July 3—two flavors, melted chocolate, nuts, even pink sprinkles, what New Yorkers call the whole schmear—knowing that I would miss my family on the Fourth, as indeed I would on Thanksgiving and Christmas too. What she did not know, but I did, was that my infant son Matthew had died on July 3, an anniversary always heralded with damned regularity by the national celebration, so that her thoughtful gift was even more welcome than usual.

I remember Kristin Urquiza speaking about her otherwise healthy sixty-five-year-old father, who died after attending a karaoke bar, who died (as she put it at the 2020 Democratic National Convention) because he supported and believed Donald Trump.[10] I honor Li Wenliang, the doctor in Wuhan who tried to warn about the pandemic and later died in it.[11] I think of Jesmyn Ward, who published a beautiful piece about her husband's death in the context of the pandemic, stressing how hearing is the last of our senses to go at death, the importance of hearing, of *being here* in the witness body.[12] As I think of them, I think as well of the 581,056 American dead, the 3.2+ million worldwide as of May 9, 2021, with totals growing daily.

Crossing Back, a book about personal loss, appears perforce in the context of national and international mourning. It presents itself to you humbly with that awareness and in that spirit, believing that individual voices can and do still reach us. *Crossing Back* narrates the death of Rose Cozzitorto De Marco, my mother, and Salvatore De Marco Jr., my brother, who lived and died before the COVID-19 crisis began or was even dreamed of. They lived and died only once, and they can be remembered but not replaced. Words from Louise DeSalvo's writing I encountered during the pandemic apply in full: "This is not something that one can prepare for, this dying of the mother, this ceasing to be of the one who gave us life, this departing of the woman whose life is so entangled with our own, so that to lose her is to lose a part of ourselves that we never acknowledged belonged to her."[13] I extend those words to the death of my fair-eyed brother Sal, my first and early playmate, who was also part of me.

The consequences of COVID-19 have been monumental for all of us, even those thus far relatively lucky and secure. They remind us of troubles likely still to come as Earth's climate changes for the worse.[14] But my mother's and brother's deaths? Those stay with me. When this book appears, there may be an effective cure and widespread, worldwide distribution of vaccines. What I write in this Prologue may evoke memories and not ongoing realities. My hope, any writer's hope, is that my words will touch you, as memoir should.

Acknowledgments

A book as long in the making as *Crossing Back* acquires a long list of debts that range from chatting and simply believing that the project would come together in the end to reading complete chapters or entire drafts.

Among friends and colleagues who have my heartfelt thanks: Kathy Pso-miades, Jan Radway, Michael Malone, Laurie Shannon, Julie Tetel, Jane Tompkins, Joe Donahue, Tsitsi Jaji, Alane Mason, Caleb Smith, and Joseph Fitzpatrick. Some of these wonderful people may not recognize the current book in discussions we had a while ago that gradually yielded the proper form.

A writing group formed during the pandemic helped me with final revisions: I'm indebted to Amin Ahmad and Taylor Black of Duke University, two generous and imaginative readers who made wonderfully specific suggestions.

Unnamed readers along the way made important suggestions, two of them for Fordham University Press and some of them on the Fordham Board. As authors do at times, I balked. But when I settled down to address the suggestions, they were always helpful and on-point. My thanks both to the readers and to the Board, as well as to Fredric Nachbaur, my editor, and to Richard Morrison, who provided some input as well. The current Prologue and the Epilogue might not have been in the book without Fordham's suggestions. Eric Newman, Rob Fellman, and the rest of the Fordham team made publication quick, efficient, and pleasant.

One earlier reader who remains anonymous objected to my involvement with yoga and meditation as a form of cultural appropriation; that seemed to me wrong-headed but helped me anticipate similar reactions and, I hope, to meet them in the spirit of peace. Or, should we say, namaste.

My husband, Stuart Torgovnick, has been, as always, incredibly supportive

of my work, as well as generously willing for me to share aspects of our lives together—a hazard of being married to any writer, but especially to a memoirist.
My daughters, Kate Torgovnick May and Elizabeth Torgovnick, appear only
fleetingly in this book, but I have thought of them throughout the writing,
hoping that my portrait of their grandmother and uncle will feel, if not totally
familiar, then ultimately right. When writing family memoirs, some warts will
out; my hope is that the love behind the book remains evident. I double that
for my nephew, Chris De Marco, whose brief appearance coincides with one
of the more painful instances in his life.

In the years it took me to complete *Crossing Back*, I was lucky indeed that
my two smart, sassy, and beautiful granddaughters were born. Although one
of them is mentioned in this book, neither appears here as fully as they do
in my heart. Italian American superstition? Perhaps. I tie a red ribbon to the
dedication that appears at the front of this book.

CROSSING BACK

Introduction

I wrote a book called *Crossing Ocean Parkway* in my thirties, telling the story of moving from a working-class Italian-American neighborhood into Jewish-American culture and then into elite colleges and universities. The book was well received and lucky enough to win an American Book Award. *Up from Bensonhurst*, I'd thought of calling it—though that title seemed too brash. I wrote it as a wife, a mother, a daughter, the child of aging parents, the sister of a conservative brother, and a native of Bensonhurst, the scene of a shocking racial murder when a group of youths shot Yusef Hawkins, a young black man on his way to look at a used car. I am still all those things, except for the child of aging parents and a sister. Adjusting to the loss of my birth family through books, family, and the process of memory itself forms the subject of this book.

Asked ten years ago, I would have said that I lived so far away from my roots that they hardly mattered. I had spent more years by then in upper-middle-class America than I had in aspiring Catholic and Jewish Brooklyn. I'd had, and have, a career in college teaching that I love. But, as I said in my earlier book, "You can take the girl out of Bensonhurst, but you cannot take the Bensonhurst out of the girl."[1] Still true. Though its racial attitudes were never mine, the cautiousness of Bensonhurst and its Italian-American love of "la bella figura"—wanting to look good in the eyes of others—still linger. What I did not know or anticipate is that, when my mother and brother died, Bensonhurst and all it meant about the past would be lost and leave me hungry. I had once yearned to cross Ocean Parkway, a symbol of upward mobility in far South Brooklyn; now I learned the impossibility crossing back, except via memory, the immigrant or exile's act and an act that was, for me, fraught with pain about the newly dead.

At age ninety, almost ninety-one, my mother developed her first and only serious illness and died shortly later from complications after surgery. When I went with her to the doctor who would perform the surgery—the first time she had ever asked me to join her—she bounded up three flights of stairs, without pausing. When he looked at her chart, he did a double-take that was not kidding or faux-gallant but surprised: "But no," he said, "you can't be ninety." She was so strong and healthy until her surgery that I thought, as many of us do, that she would last forever. Her decline happened over a period of weeks, not years, in a far quicker version of "the end" than granted many.

Her hospitalization and death took me back to Brooklyn—to her hospital in Borough Park, to a funeral home on West Sixth Street, and to a burial in Greenwood Cemetery—followed by the painful ritual of clearing out her things and the terra incognita of how much her late-life partner, Joe, should remain in my life. It confronted me, more abruptly than we ever anticipate, with loss and the change from being the child of a living mother to being the mother of grown children and, as people say, "at the head of the line." From feeling amused by my parents to feeling bereft and wishing, as legions have before me, that I could see them again, if only for a day, and hear their rough-hewn wisdom. The change of finding Bensonhurst, which I once said "never changed"—accurate enough back then—had changed, a lot.

Where Italian- and Jewish-Americans once lived, Chinese and Chinese-American families live now in the same modest one-to-four-family houses, often occupied, as is the custom, by branches of the same family. When "the Chinese"—always a stereotype in this context—bought her building, they evicted my mother's partner Joe from his downstairs apartment, and she felt forced to leave as well, though she had, as he did not, the iron-clad protection of what New York calls rent control. It was my mother's first move since her marriage to my father in 1942 and one that took her, at age eighty-eight, no further than one flight down and to the building next door.

Italian and Chinese immigrants share certain hard-knock attitudes toward life; they also share old-world habits, like the daily washing of sidewalks. When the mothers in Amy Tan's *The Joy Luck Club* make jokes about strangling a rooster, it reminds me of one of my mother's favorite quips about feeding the family pig in Calabria, Italy, and then serving it as food. "I liked the pig when I fed it," she'd say, "and I liked it even better when I ate its meat." She'd tell this story when she served sausage in her Sunday gravy and sometimes add, in her sardonic way, that she liked the sausage best of all.

With Asian food more common now in Bensonhurst than Italian sausages or Jewish knishes, a once-bustling "pork store" on West Sixth Street—a source of cheese, meat, and classic cold cuts—looks lonely. On Eighty-Sixth Street, once a great Italian-American shopping boulevard and outdoor market, I struggle now to find a cappuccino and Italian pastries. I once feared that I would be "banished forever from the land of *cremolata*," a vanilla-almond-flavored ice usually eaten after dinner (*COP*, 18). Instead, the land of *cremolata* has withdrawn to strongholds like Eighteenth Avenue in Brooklyn or moved farther west, to Staten Island and New Jersey.

Memoir is about the living—how not?—and the process of being alive. But the experience of death often motivates its writing. In fact, memoir arises quite often from the vulnerability of grief and offers itself to the world as honestly as it can—in this case, as the Prologue says, with a full and humble awareness of COVID-19's tragic path. *Crossing Back* tells the story of grief for my birth family, a grief acknowledged almost unwillingly, that could only be confronted over time. While its emotions are personal, sometimes intensely so, others will, I believe, recognize them too.

My mother—my Mama, I find myself calling her now, though I never did while she lived—appeared without knowing it as a character in *Crossing Ocean Parkway*, where she played a secondary or even tertiary role, mostly making short ironic comments characteristic of the way she spoke. My father was the star parent in that earlier book—the reader among my parents and so the one I saw as the most supportive of the education I craved. He worked in Manhattan and took me to what we called "the City," encouraging my awareness of its pulse. I remember wearing his hat as a young child and carrying a bag and saying that one day I'd work in the City too and be his secretary. My parents laughed, since bank messengers, my father's job, do not have secretaries.

My father was also the parent who died as I completed *Crossing Ocean Parkway*, "forcing me," as I say there—a locution I now find strange—"to make peace." It was natural that he took center stage in that book. *Crossing Back* tells the story of a different time of life, what I'll gently call full maturity—a period of large-scale family loss and change but also, in the end, of continuity. It is, quite naturally, anchored by my mother.

Although she was born in New York, my mother, Rose, was sent back to the rural toe of Italy's boot with her mother and raised there with her siblings until age sixteen. She never went to school or had an American education, and she was fearful that college would take me out of familiar ways. On the surface, she wanted me to work in an office or, at most, to be an elementary school teacher so that I would marry in and stay close to "the neighborhood." Yet I always seem to have had money for plays and subway fare to go to Manhattan, and my brother and I were the first among our cousins to go to college—surely no accident. My father was the one who played math games and helped us with homework, for as long as he could, since he only finished the eighth grade. But, in our family, a covert matriarchy, college would not have happened without my mother's consent. To her dying day, I feel sure that my mother remained proudest not of my education or career, which she articulated as "teaching teachers," but of her two granddaughters. She perhaps understood my place in the world as a tenured professor only after she attended their college graduations and felt the kind of plush, pleasant life major universities can offer. "They gave us so much food," she said admiringly on both occasions, "and for free."

The aftereffects of my mother's death lasted for years, even, I'd say now, for a full decade, prolonged by my initial unwillingness to grieve and by my brother's fatal cancer. I sought consolation and even joy in reading and writing on books and family and committed to a daily meditation practice in yoga traditions that I consider American practices too: Ishta Yoga, founded by Alan Finger, a Jewish yogi from South Africa who makes no claim to be a guru, and Integral Yoga, founded by Swami Sachadinanda, who came to America expressly to bring his traditions to the United States. Ishta has more of the features one associates with yoga, American style, by which I mean teachers who are generally lithe and long of limb and who show some concern for fashion and style. Integral is what's called Bhakti or service yoga: Instructors teach for free and come in all shapes and sizes; at an Integral class, it's hard to underdress.

Both share a deep and pervasive emphasis on meditation as something that should accompany yoga from day one, regardless of physical ability. Though these traditions route, like all yoga, through Indian genealogies, I consider them American as well as South Asian, and I do not consider them what some purists might call cultural appropriation. In fact, as the author of an earlier book called *Gone Primitive* that castigates Western uses of tribal cultures, the possible charge of cultural appropriation—which I have heard—makes me marvel at things that go around and come around.

As in my earlier memoir, I follow my writing where it takes me—allowing a certain freedom as I go and not telling the story slavishly in chronological order. Reading great books, I feel better or, at least, feel that the experience of reading and studying opens me up to mourning, a process I constitutionally resisted as somehow shameful. I take some journeys that seem to further the mourning process, which I know by now will have no quick end. Then, after my brother dies, I reenter grief, read or reread other classic books, and begin to write about them in what feels like a mid- to late-life Bildungsroman.

Cumulatively, by revisiting aspects of my past, I reclaim memory, calming emotions that made me something other than myself for years: a riled-up creature who moved restlessly from place to place and could not seem to finish projects I began. Through a series of meditations on childhood and on places I have lived, the final chapters in this book explore what Roland Barthes calls memory without "the pain of absence."[2] That concept is related to meditation, since almost all meditation practices advise allowing thoughts to cross the mind but to think of them as "movies" or "maya" (illusion) and to witness them with a detachment that distances depression or pain.

If you are looking for a detailed guide to the classics, *Crossing Back* is not that book. Though it does contain compact theories and some close readings, its chapters invite you to read the classics rather than show that I have done so. If you are looking for a flat-out grief memoir, this is not that book either, since it places grief within larger contexts. Instead, *Crossing Back* is intended to be, as its subtitle promises, a warm and intimate user's guide to books, family, and memory in the mourning process, the endpoint being memory without pain and the users being not just me, but us.

Rituals

The anthropologist Renato Rosaldo tells a personal story that I have never been able to forget. He was researching the Ilongot, a headhunting tribe in the remote Philippines, when his wife, Michelle, slipped and fell sixty-five feet down a mountain. After making the descent, Rosaldo discovered her body, lifeless, as feared.

Thrust into a state of mourning that deepened all the way to despair, Rosaldo was for a time unable to work. Fifteen months passed. Then, when he reopened the notes he had taken among the headhunters, something astonishing happened.

He and Michelle had begun to focus on why the Ilongot headhunt and how recent government prohibitions had affected them. When asked why they headhunt and if they missed doing so, his informants gave long, dry, genealogical lists of ancestry, kin, and the places they had lived and gardened. They seemed to resist, or at least not to understand, the self-reflection Rosaldo wanted. But now, after his own bereavement, Rosaldo suddenly understood that the Ilongot had answered his questions and answered them quite concisely.

The Ilongot headhunt to create a feeling of buoyancy and renewal during mourning, and its absence had left them without customary release. They responded by affirming kinship lines and marking places they had lived and grown their food. Recitations of family names and familiar sites replaced headhunting to balance what Rosaldo calls "the emotional force of a death . . . an intimate relation's permanent rupture."[3] Their recitations nourished their souls much as their traditional gardens had fed their bodies and their ancestral practices had lifted their spirits.

What do the Ilongot have in common with the role of books, family, and memory at a time of loss? In a surprising way, almost everything.

When my strong Italian-American mother died, followed much too soon by my brother, my only sibling, their deaths abruptly marked the end of my birth family. Although I have a husband and children of my own, I found myself brittle, irritable, and unable to finish projects for a surprisingly long time. Because my losses seemed normal, natural, and even quotidian, I remained numbly cut off from grief and yet, somehow, submerged in it, with each push toward cheerfulness repulsed.

Shortly before these deaths, I had written about World War II in *The War Complex*, a book that immersed me in large and even overwhelming facts. Fifty to eighty million people killed, most of them civilians, the devastation so enormous that estimates still vary that widely. Whole families snuffed out, sometimes over years, sometimes in minutes. Around the same time historically, and forming part of my material, satellite disasters like Stalin's purges, partition in India, and revolution in China uprooted and killed millions more, sometimes under government auspices. I was writing about somber stuff, anything but cheery.

As disasters piled up in our own century—earthquakes, tsunamis, hurricanes, famine, drought, fires, the impending doom of climate change, wars, refugees, unwelcome migrants, deep political divisiveness—it seemed like the world and I were sharing a mood. As I revised *Crossing Back* for publication, the COVID-19 pandemic kept us at home, and we saw both racial tensions and a frayed America. But way before 2020, the constellation of facts and feelings already made it hard for me to acknowledge my personal grief. Like Dorothea Brooke in George Eliot's *Middlemarch*, I wanted to be highminded: Amid such wholesale devastation, how could I claim my personal grief? Hadn't I learned a larger view regarding what Susan Sontag calls "the pain of others"?[4] Shouldn't I shoulder my load and, like billions of others, soldier on? Grieving seemed impossible, monomaniacal—the microcosm challenging the universe. And yet, as I was aware all the time, I could not choose my grief, because my grief had chosen me.

I used to call my mother every Sunday in the perfunctory way many of us do, asking and answering the same questions about relatives, health, food, the weather. Now I found myself wanting to shout out across time: Ma—how long do I cook the sauce for the pasta, and do I brown the meatballs first? Or, equally small but the kind of thing my mother always knew, how many fifty-two-inch curtains to cover a 116-inch window? Or, more pointedly, Ma, where in Sicily did Dad's family live? What was the name of the tiny village where you grew up? I can Google the meatballs and the measurements, but the more personal questions echo, forever unanswered.

After each of these two deaths, epochal for me but what we call in common parlance "natural," I participated in traditional forms of Italian-American mourning. I sat nightly at the funeral home, receiving relatives and neighbors and thanking them for coming. I attended an impersonal Mass at the local parish church, taking communion once I was assured that it would no longer be considered a mortal sin if I sincerely wished to do so. (Complicated, always, a lapsed Catholic's relationship to mortal sin.) I attended burials in northern New Jersey for my brother and in Brooklyn's prestigious Greenwood Cemetery for my mother—in her case, near the entrance and by the fence, a site my parents no doubt chose as relatively inexpensive and also (a bonus) accessible by bus, rather than by car, which they did not own.

"Look at him displayed up there, all stuffed and ridiculous. When I go, I don't want any of this," a cousin's wife said at my brother's funeral. She too had cancer and died the following year, close in time to yet another cousin, two aunts, and an uncle—a surplus of mortality in the family. My cousin's wife had a point. Like me, my brother would have found the whole occasion funny, if we could have shared the joke.

Not surprising, then, that none of the traditional Catholic practices worked as healing rituals. Instead, I shuttled restlessly from place to place—changing houses in North Carolina for the first time in twenty-four years and moving every three years in New York, where I also live. A coincidence, I told myself. A pragmatic matter of downsizing in Carolina while I sought better apartments in New York, as people do. The moves kept me busy—very much so. But then, when reading Roland Barthes's *Mourning Diary*, I recognized my motives as less pragmatic and more inchoate than I'd thought.

My mother and brother, who had always been there, now were not. Under the rupture of one of life's intimate relations—in my case, two—I entered a spiritual and psychological state I had written about as a critic, one that the theorist Georg Lukács calls "transcendental homelessness": the feeling of being truly at home nowhere, of being spiritually adrift. In a grand act of symbolic reenactment, I moved repeatedly and, as my mother would say, "kept busy."

Over time, I discovered that a third death colored and prolonged my feelings of grief: my first child Matthew's death in infancy, which, in the course of a happier lifetime, had never been adequately acknowledged. My new losses told me that I needed to take stock of my son's death too. Reading and meditating, followed by writing, became daily healing rituals. Other people choose different paths: religion, physical transformation, lifelong dedication to preserving the memory of the dead, learning a new and even esoteric skill connected to the beloved, therapy. All good. Meditations on books, family, and memory itself served as healing rituals for me.

Classic Turns

I felt virtuous and original when I turned to classic books in a time of grief—like a student earning a gold star. Then I realized that many bookish people do that too. Sigmund Freud, Georg Lukács, Walter Benjamin, Max Horkheimer, and Theodor Adorno; recent writers like Joseph Lizzi, Helen MacDonald, and Daniel Mendelsohn. It's a long and illustrious, though partial, list. Do great books work under such conditions? And, if so, how?

Homer, Sophocles, Aeschylus, Euripides, Vergil, Dante, Shakespeare, Milton, with selective additions from Flaubert to Faulkner, Woolf to Nabokov, Atwood to McEwan. Unrolling over centuries, with variations mostly after 1800, that stable list provides, in and of itself, a majestic and consoling sense of order. That's part of the undeniable appeal of classic books. Accordingly, most books about reading proceed chronologically or impose some other rigid sequencing that controls arbitrary flux. I think of twenty-first-century authors of mourning memoirs like Christopher Beha, who made the idiosyncratic choice to read, one by one, his grandmother's shelf of the Harvard Great Books. Or Nina Sankovitch, who whimsically chose library books that could be read in a single day. Other writers on the classics, like Harold Bloom, pick a center or several centers—in Bloom's case Shakespeare—and survey the canon from it. *In a Dark Wood*, by my fellow Italian-American Joseph Luzzi, found special meaning in Dante's *Divine Comedy*. Even Helen MacDonald's wonderful *H Is for Hawk* anchors her own adventures in the fantasist J. R. R. Tolkien's diaries.[5]

Usually seen as fonts of wisdom and generally described as "bright and shining," the classics aren't primarily sparkly at all.[6] Instead, they address war, grief, loss, and family matters of the darkest kind, often in conjunction—so that the classic turn comes less from an elevated state of mind than from the desire to feel reassured amid instability. My work on "the primitive" had familiarized me with headhunting tribes like the Ilongot, in which men sleep on their fathers' skulls and, in analogous actions, take enemy heads and store them. Bookish people collect classics much as tribal headhunters collect heads: to lighten and remedy the volatile emotions that death introduces into ordinary lives. To ground experience in the context of the past.

Almost by definition, it's hard to match the classics or even to imagine trying to do so. They have what the critic Walter Benjamin called an *aura* of uniqueness and authenticity that separates them from modern reproduction and the simulacra so easily found on our cell phones.[7] Even a fine digital re-production—and those can be very fine indeed—will never have the aura of, say, Monet's *Water Lilies* or even a quick, small drawing by Picasso. Whether traditionally Greek or Roman, Renaissance, modern, or contemporary, all classic books—and I say this without cherry picking—concern war, mortal-ity, mourning, humanity's flaws, and the limitations of language. They deal with "dark" themes commonly effaced in idealized, celebratory views. Classic books inspire more than a pleasant afterglow: They channel our emotions.[8]

In fact, classic stories beget other classic stories and form, like us, a living tissue. Great books don't reject updated versions like David Malouf's *Ransom* or Madeline Miller's *Circe*; they don't mind personal readings in memoirs.[9] In fact, they invite and welcome them. Classic tales echo with our lives in our nurseries, in our loves and marriages, and around our holiday tables. Their permeability with our lives forms, I believe, a source of their continuing power.

Ordering Flux

Gregorian chants, prayer rituals, Sufi trances, Buddhist reflection, mindful-ness and mantras. Like great books, meditation practices root back through long and sometimes ancient traditions and establish a sense of context, order, and balance. They involve gradual steps, proscribed sequences, and regular-ity that quiet and still the mind, countering the sense that life is, ultimately, arbitrary flux. At their most intense, they transcend time.

Though some meditation traditions derive from the East rather than from Europe or the United States, they now form important parts of Western and American culture too, so much so that I remain unmoved by charges of cul-tural appropriation. In fact, I can think of no true yogi, no true spiritual teacher of any kind, who would object to being adopted by others. Appropriation, if you will, is what spiritual teachers, much like classic stories, want and do.

Just as, almost by definition, it's hard to rival great books, it's hard to write about meditation without sounding hyperbolic or loopy—all flowers, baby kittens, namaste, and starry light. It's also difficult to describe the goal of med-itation, which quite simply yet also quite profoundly is a temporary sense of stepping away from the self and an awareness of eternity. I've written about the *oceanic*, a similar phenomenon, in some of my work and traced its role in, for example, writers like Virginia Woolf and some ecstatic traditions within primitivism.[10] To tame my grief, I turned to meditation, and, like reading clas-sic books, it worked psychologically and even, medicine tells us, physically.

Meditation places tumultuous feelings into larger contexts, witnessing grief and nurturing memory without pain.

Just as classic literature tends to be idealized, meditation has become surprisingly trendy and hip—practiced by a variety of often well-heeled others rather than by solitary ascetics. Upscale houses can now feature meditation rooms stocked with attractive pillows and props; urban centers have glitzy meditation palaces that seem a contradiction in terms. No such props are necessary for mediation, which can take place anywhere and anytime, even in a car or plane.

The deeply cynical usually do not try to meditate, but most people who do agree that it works. "What *was* that?" novices sometimes ask after a meditation session; "what happened when the instructor walked around the room?" As we emerged from a well-seasoned meditation space, one newbie man said to me, marveling, "That was amazing. It felt like my grandmother was in there." I replied, only half-jokingly, "Maybe she was," and then, more seriously, "lots of energy in that room." In fact, in meditation, something organic and transformative happens that we dismiss as a placebo at our peril.

Surprisingly, then, point-by-point comparisons exist between reading great books and meditation as healing rituals. Lineage and tradition willingly accepted; regularity, sequencing, and order imposed upon flux; connection to larger entities that gives a calming perspective on recent events. In putting reading and meditation together, I was onto something—something I wanted to share.

PART I
Facing Grief

1
Living Tissue

A classic is something that tends to relegate the concerns of the moment to background noise, but at the same time this background noise is something we cannot do without.

— ITALO CALVINO

Knowing, as I do, that I am likely to die of cancer, a biography of the dreaded disease gets my attention.[1] The illness that we fight and battle and cut and burn and inject poisons to purge remains, at its core, unsettlingly like ourselves. "Cell division allows us as organisms to grow, to adapt, to recover, to repair, to live," the author writes. "Cancer is a flaw in our growth, but this flaw is deeply entrenched." What's more, and worse, cancer cells "grow faster, adapt better" than we do. "More perfect versions of ourselves," they are "survival-endowed, scrappy, fecund, inventive."[2] The words bear repeating: Cancers are scrappy, fecund, inventive—more perfect versions of ourselves.[3]

When *The Emperor of All Maladies* came out, I read reviews but didn't want to read the book—it was too close to home and to how my family dies. Once I gave in and started, I couldn't stop. I wanted to process its unflinching words but could not just then, perhaps because I have to hope that a personal encounter with invasive cancer, if it comes, remains many years away. Still, *The Emperor of All Maladies* gave me pause. Having been experienced, it could not be "unexperienced" or forgotten.[4]

"Living Tissue" once meant to me that, like us, great books grow and change over time—with us, and then beyond our lifetimes. That's still true. But after *The Emperor of All Maladies* appeared, the phrase acquired a different meaning. Great myths and stories form scrappy, fecund, inventive, hyperbolic versions of our lives. They multiply by attracting later versions, other stories. They form, like us, living tissue. Was my intuition also a memory?

Having begun to read classic books and to meditate after my mother died, having traveled on yoga journeys and begun to settle down emotionally, I learned that, despite longevity in the family we had begun to take for granted, my brother was dying from pancreatic cancer, "the epitome of the dismal," even within the dispiriting world of cancer (Mukherjee, *Emperor*, 154). All bets were off.

I carried on as usual as much as possible, among many other things going to see a South African play called *Molora*, which bills itself as a contemporary version of Aeschylus's *Oresteia*. Though my writing already had a personal spin, very curiously, or so it seems to me now, I did not think of myself and my brother at all as I watched the play. Months later, when I wrote about it, I reexperienced it as the only sister to my only brother.

Something Once Experienced Can Be Reexperienced

Stone-faced, an aged woman dressed in calico responded to my request to pass her at the end of the row with just a slight adjustment of her body.[5] In her silence, strength, and impressiveness, she made me think of my mother. I'd come to see *Molora*, a modern play produced in South Africa and based on Aeschylus's ancient trilogy, the *Oresteia*.[6] Though the woman sat in the audience, she avoided eye contact and was so unusually dressed that I suspected she was an actor in the play—most likely an avenging Fury.

Molora expands the classic narrative I remember vividly from my reading of the *Oresteia* as an undergraduate—three plays that stunned me by their audacity in explaining how Greek culture moved from blood vengeance to the rule of law. Like the Oedipus cycle, the *Oresteia's* three plays—*Agamemnon*, *The Libation Bearers*, and *The Eumenides*—chronicle family misdeeds and their consequences, in this case concerning the Trojan War and its aftermath. But, like cancer, the story's roots extend back further and deeper. Here's a short summary of the *Oresteia* for those who would value one.

Pledged to support his brother Menelaus, whose wife Helen had been abducted by Troy's Prince Paris, the Greek commander Agamemnon finds his ships stalled at Aulis: the wind calm, prophecies say, until the gods receive a human sacrifice. The commander lures his daughter Iphigenia to his troops under the pretense that she will wed the hero Achilles before the Greek ships sail. Instead, "Hoist . . . over the altar, like a yearling," she has her throat cut to bring the winds (*Agamemnon*, ll. 216–37). Wound tight with hatred, her mother Clytemnestra yearns for vengeance over ten long years. She takes a lover named Aegisthus, in some legends her husband's cousin, in others, his half-brother, begotten by incest. (Like memoir, Greek myth includes repetitions that open trapdoors of meaning.) In Agamemnon's absence, Aegisthus rules as makeshift king.[7] On his return, Agamemnon is lulled and coddled, soothed and bathed. Then, while he lies naked and defenseless, Clytemnestra traps him in a net, murders him with an axe, and buries him without royal honors. Cassandra, Troy's doleful princess and Agamemnon's war prize, shares his fate. Ever prophetic, she laments it in advance.

In *Molora*—just the recent play now, no longer Aeschylus—Klytemnestra tells us that she herself was Agamemnon's captive once and made his wife after the murder of her first husband and young baby. (In *Molora*, her name is spelled with a *K*, offering a convenient way to differentiate the South African play from its ancient model. I follow *Molora*'s spelling of Klytemnestra and Elektra only in instances where the action in *Molora* diverges from its source or when referencing only the recent play.) Over time, Klytemnestra's two dead children—the unnamed first and Iphigenia—have merged in her mind. The text of *Molora* gives the source of this codicil to the story as "unknown," but simple research showed that it's a standard variation on the myth and an entirely plausible addition.

We tend to think of the ancient Greeks as civilized aesthetes, the inventors of democracy. On that basis, many critics of the classics idealize the Greeks as symbols of harmony and grace. But Agamemnon and his brother Menelaus lived like pirates and had just begun to establish the greater permanence of empire.[8] The golden relic called Agamemnon's Mask, found in Mycenae and exhibited now in Athens, captures the mix of civilization and savagery typical of the period when the Greek epics are set. The characters who populate the epics lived by plunder, conquest, rape, and enslavement, and those deeds run deep in the legends behind the *Oresteia* and *Molora*. Clytemnestra's marriage to Agamemnon and all their children stem from brutal acts in the immediate past, just as her husband's lineage leads back through the house of Atreus and actions such as patricide, the taunting of the gods, and the eating of children. Such a terrifying list of ancestral deeds is not unusual in Greek myth.[9]

After Agamemnon's murder, his daughter Electra too has something she will never forget. That's basic both to the original Aeschylus and to *Molora*. But while Electra's grief forms only a small part of Aeschylus's cycle, it moves front and center in the South African tale.

Molora's Elektra (another *k* to distinguish the two characters) has waited seventeen years since her father's death, when she hid her brother Orestes with two loyal servants. She has long anticipated his return and their joint revenge.[10] More and more obsessed by the need to find and kill Orestes before he can avenge his father, *Molora*'s Klytemnestra visits her bile on her daughter.

"I'll get it out of you," I hear Klytemnestra say onstage, "An eye for an eye, blood for blood, and a tooth for a tooth," she intones as she swaggers, larger and more powerful than her daughter—a red dressing gown swinging open at her hips, a lit cigarette dangling. She sounds like the Old Testament God or, more to the point, like the blood vengeance that she, her children, and the Furies all represent (*Molora*, 33, 45). In the recent play, we see Klytemnestra burn Elektra with cigarettes and beat her; we see her plunge her daughter's head into water and hold it there. We see her cover Elektra's face with a plastic bag and pull it taut, all the while casually smoking. A mini-Auschwitz, a theatrical Abu Ghraib.

In Aeschylus's ancient *Oresteia*, egged on by his sister, Orestes murders his mother.[11] The Furies then pursue Orestes, but a court of law finds him innocent because the father's seed gives life, making the need to avenge parricide trump matricide, or so the goddess Athena argues, having herself been born from Zeus's head. The court sides half with Athena and half with the Furies, which requires Athena to break the tie in favor of Orestes. In compensation, the Furies receive the Underworld as their dominion.

To this mythic narrative, already extraordinary in its power, the Farber Foundry of South Africa added yet another rich dimension and inserted surprising twists.

Brothers and Sisters

I saw this play during the season of my brother's illness, a period when we both knew that he was dying even though he was responding well to chemotherapy. In fact, my brother seemed to be in remission, and so we both drifted in the space of a particularly terrible mortal illness where everything seemed stable, in a time that might be ongoing. We hoped, as do so many characters in Greek tragedy, that "all may yet be well"—though we knew it wouldn't. It was early spring, a time of hope. Mid-fall, he told me that he had pancreatic cancer.

I was at a restaurant when I heard the news, on Erev Yom Kippur with my husband and our older daughter before they began their fast, making it easy to date the event. Sal called rarely—in fact, never—so his message almost surely signaled an emergency. I returned his call immediately. As Sal spoke, I took notes to process his words amid the restaurant's noise and thought, somehow, that he'd said "prostate cancer." At the end of our conversation, I felt flattened to see the words "pancreatic cancer" on the page instead.

"Did you say prostate or pancreatic?"

"Pancreatic."

It was, we both knew, a death sentence. .

A long conversation later that night told me more. The cancer had spread to his liver, eliminating surgery as an option. For some months, he had been involved in a series of tests, MRIs, and scores that go up and down. He had entered Cancer World.[12] For reasons he did not explain, he didn't want to call me until his wife insisted. Did he feel some strange sense of shame, typical of our family, that he was not "doing well"? He kept repeating, mistakenly, that this particular cancer has a strong hereditary link, meaning that his son and I should be tested immediately and often.[13] (There is, in fact, no reliable test beyond checking for the sudden onset of diabetes. In addition, the hereditary link is possible but not necessarily strong.)

In legend, Electra is the older of the two siblings. It was the reverse for us—my brother, my only sibling, two years my senior. In the small Brooklyn apartment where our family lived, just three subway stops from Coney Island, we shared a room until puberty and forged a joint imaginative life filled with stories based on TV: war documentaries, especially World War II; cowboy shows like *Wagon Train* and *Bonanza*; the adventure show *Sky King*, with the fearless girl pilot Penny; *The Buccaneers*. Imaginative children, we'd discuss these shows in the darkness of the night from our separate beds. The next day we'd devise scripts and act them out, just the two of us, or joined by friends or cousins.

Like many small two-to-four-family houses in far South Brooklyn, ours was attached to another on one side but had a space, an alley, on the other that formed our playground. I remember war plots and gangsters, or cowboys and Indians, played in improvised foxholes and forts. The only girl, and younger than the rest, I was usually an early victim—shot, scalped, and forgotten while the boys got to be macho and play on. These childhood games form, I'm pretty sure, the reason that I gravitate toward gangster, war, and cowboy films even now—such masculine genres. Though playing so often with boys, I was not a tomboy. But I continued to be strongly male identified, with many men as friends, and did not bond as easily with women until later in life, when I had children.[14]

What does this sibling history have to do with *Molora*? Not much, I would have said when I saw it on the stage. Now I have to identify some willful repression or denial here—the kind that lets you carry on in times of trouble. Because today I'd say, a lot.

My brother and I grew apart during college and as adults. Our politics differed, our lifestyles, our values. Sal was a chemical engineer turned salesman of engineering supplies. He either got bored with his original work or (I thought this at the time) wanted to have less income on the books while he paid alimony after his first divorce. A hard-smoking, hard-drinking Republican, he had three marriages and two messy divorces yet never, ever, talked to me about his personal or emotional life.

I became a professor, a classic liberal, and someone who always identified strongly with New York. I've been married to the same man for decades and have two daughters my brother liked—I think somewhat grudgingly, for he and my husband always tolerated rather than enjoyed each other's company. After age twenty, our parents formed our strongest bond and common purpose. When we came together, it was to take action for our father or our mother. But as kids, Sal and I were really close.

We would find our Christmas presents when our parents were at work, neatly rewrapping them so they wouldn't know. In elementary school, we'd carefully set fires in the bathroom sink, erasing every trace by 5 PM. "I don't want to set the world on fire," we would sing to each other before dinner was served, giggling at the table. In middle and high school, we remained friends, with his friends also mine—though I got relegated more and more to the role of kid sister.

Once my brother entered college, our closeness ended. He joined the ROTC (withdrawing, as it happened, before he'd be committed to serve); I dated a ROTC friend of his once but hated the vibe. We grew apart. Once I went to New York University, a radical haven, the rift grew wider and soon permanent. My mother always worried about what would happen to our relationship once she died. She was both correct and incorrect to do so. For the strange thing, and it happened twice, around each parent's health, was how quickly we'd respond to the call of blood and common childhoods. When our parents needed us, we could reaccess easily our early closeness. Despite our very different values, we saw things the same way for many years without a hesitation or a stutter.

When my father was diagnosed with lung cancer, we reacted pragmatically and methodically, as our upbringing had taught. We both went with our father to his doctor, where, being of a different generation, Dad expected not to be told the truth. "It's bad, isn't it," he said rather than asked—using the same words I'd heard him use decades earlier when told his beloved niece Marion's cancer had metastasized—and adding: "Level with me." But the doctor had told us exactly what he had told my father, so that we had nothing to reveal—six months, maybe a year, a figure that often, as one learns, turns out to be shorter.

As things got worse and my parents sought advice about end-of-life directives and hospices, my brother and I made decisions easily together on the phone or in person. I helped both parents draw up living wills—they asked me, not him, a fact that became significant later. Well into the process, I began to write to cope, and I'm pretty sure my brother would have been annoyed or even angry with me had he known.[15] Other than that, we were tight, unified, like Orestes and Electra, who also come together for their parents after much time spent apart. The same easily shared values reemerged at first when my mother got ill but changed after her surgery led to a stroke.

Getting Our Humanity Back

When control of South Africa passed in 1994 from minority-White to majority-Black Africans, the company that produced *Molora* saw analogies between its nation's recent history and Aeschylus's *Oresteia*. At that time, the program notes tell us, "the world held its collective breath in anticipation of a civil war that would surely unleash the rage of generations shattered by the Apartheid Regime."[16] Violence did erupt—an epidemic of rape, for instance, reflected in books like J. M. Coetzee's *Disgrace* and in statistics from the late 1990s. Crime flared in major cities and still does sometimes today, though South Africa has made itself into a major tourist destination. Still, in the decade after Apartheid's end, peace and forgiveness unexpectedly burst out too.

Truth and Reconciliation panels held around the nation allowed for public statements and reenactments of guilt and grief, marked by ritual chanting by Whites and Blacks, oppressors and oppressed, murderers and the survivors of those killed. The complex process blended White and Black traditions in a heartfelt way, without rote enactment.

The mother of a murdered man captures the moment well when she ponders the meaning of "Truth and Reconciliation." "This thing called Reconciliation," she says, "If I am understanding it correctly . . . if it means the perpetrator, this man who has killed my son, if it means he becomes human again, this man, so that I, so that all of us, get our humanity back . . . then I agree, then I support it all" ("Adaptor-Director's Note").[17] Her words recall the founding principle of the Truth and Reconciliation Commission: *ubuntu*, a Zulu word translated by the phrase "a person is a person through other persons."[18] The phrase echoes with what Christians call the Golden Rule and with similar principles found in many traditions. Truth and Reconciliation's version embodies justice through group actions.

Lights up, with me in the audience, the play began. An older woman, dressed like the one at the end of my row, began chanting, lumbered down the aisle, and walked onto the stage. "*Iaphala igazi*" ("blood has been spilt"), her summons ran, calling the elders to judgment. Their only utterances came in Xhosa split-tone song, in rhythmic dance, and in strong emotive gestures from their native Transkei.[19] Knowing *Molora*'s ancient model and its South African roots, I guessed by the middle of the play the destination of Truth and Reconciliation. But matricide and pursuit by the Furies seems so inevitable in Aeschylus's original that I did not think that *Molora* could make reconciliation work. And then, somehow, it did.

Onstage, the Chorus listened to Elektra and witnessed her suffering. It heard as well what Clytemnestra had to say. It seemed to approve Orestes's murder of Aegisthus, seeing it, much as Homer's *Odyssey* does, simply as a son's setting his father's house in order. But then, holding the weapon and poised to murder his mother, *Molora*'s Orestes hesitated, and the Chorus encouraged his change of heart, advocating for Klytemnestra's life more effectively than she did. For though Klytemnestra angled for mercy, she remained surprisingly passive and under the spell of the moment, half courting death. Members of the Chorus had come to hear, to see, to empathize—but also to heal. With words and gestures, when they saw their opening in Orestes's hesitation, they took it.[20]

Within the Ngqoko cultural group that formed the Chorus "are two spiritual diviners, who are trained in the channeling of ancestral powers" (program notes). They did not go into "authentic trance" on stage—that could only happen within their communities. Still, at the play's climactic moment, as they supported Orestes and affirmed his becalming, the audience felt their authority. Then, when a still-furious Elektra picked up Orestes's weapon to strike, they embraced her. She fought them off and would not relinquish the chance to kill her mother until physically surrounded by the entire group and actively restrained.

Once violence was arrested—swiftly, almost magically, but quite convincingly—the group faced the audience. A bundle hanging above the stage opened, covering them with ash, the meaning of *molora*. Then, in the production I saw, they marched in procession into the audience: the Ngqoko Chorus, mixed with the woman in red playing Klytemnestra, mixed with Elektra and Orestes,[21] echoing the procession that ended yearly performances of Aeschylus's trilogy in ancient Athens.[22] It formed a triumphant moment, a tremendous surge that transformed Aeschylus's plot while respecting its potent symbolism. From a narrative about forms of justice—blood lust, matricide, and vengeance versus communal law—*Molora*'s version of the *Oresteia* sang a hymn to the power of group ritual to effect purgation. Yet *Molora* did not claim too much. Klytemnestra and Orestes remained streaked with blood; Elektra seemed calmed but not healed.

"*Unogquevela*" ("handicapped"), the recessional chant said, marking how something (innocence, love, familial bonds) had been irremediably lost but also marking the possibility of continuing. Brilliantly and before our eyes, the performance juxtaposed two very different situations—the ancient *Oresteia* and the recent Truth and Reconciliation panels—and made both feel real. We had before us, simultaneously, the classic and the contemporary.[23] I could see and feel that, powerfully. What I could not see, at first, was the personal invitation the play extended.

Handicapped

My brother was always, or so it seemed to me, my mother's favorite child. "But he's the boy," my mother would say, when I protested what seemed like special treatment. She might have been joking and sometimes no doubt was, but at other times, she spoke what to her was the simple truth, rooted in the logic of her culture. She loved her daughter. But her son, in this case also her first child, was extra special. I accepted the situation, though it generated my first inchoate doubts that men were really so great.

My parents supported my brother Sal's decision to withdraw from the ROTC after two years so that he would not have to go into the army. Vietnam was on, and a neighbor's son, an early playmate in our war games, had come back dead; that probably played its part. I remember the suspense while we waited to hear whether Brooklyn Polytech (his private college, now part of NYU) would increase his scholarship; it did. My parents did not complain when Sal borrowed money to buy his first car to drive to work in New Jersey and never paid them back, despite the fact that he was becoming middle class and they had very little.

My mother's only doubts about my brother surfaced during his divorces. He divorced twice, and she was conflicted, wanting to believe that he was right but also ashamed he'd left his first wife and child for a woman he'd met in a bar who, years later, left him. She found an explanation only an Italian-American could love. Sal's first wife, she concluded, left her meat in the freezer too long: "Six months. She'd just forget about it. And the meat would be all white and burned—no good."

She couldn't understand how divorce could happen in our family once, much less twice. It was hard on her, made easier only by similar disasters among some cousins. In the end, my mother never told the family about my brother's third marriage. At my father's funeral, she insisted to our friends and relatives that my brother's third wife was really his second—brushing off anyone who noticed the difference in names or appearance by claiming that "Debbie" had gained weight, dyed her hair from blonde to red, and started using her middle name. I'm not sure anyone believed her, but like good Italian-Americans, they never said.

My mother and brother got through the divorces with their bond intact. But they couldn't get past Joe, her late-life partner. No one had killed my father; no need for vengeance burned. But my brother reacted with the rage of an Orestes when, four years after my father died, my mother had a new man in her life. Short, while my father had been tall, Joe was Sicilian born and spoke in heavily accented English; my father had been American and fairly well spoken. Joe had been in the military—in Libya, for Mussolini, during World War II, which I found amazing. Mild mannered, playful, neatly and well dressed, a barber by trade and extremely easy going, Joe differed from my father, whose pride bruised easily and who always hid his feminine side. My father did the dishes and ironed the clothing with the blinds closed; Joe did "women's work" quite openly. My mother's relationship with Joe was a love match my brother just couldn't accept, a glowing decade in extreme old age when my mother acted with all the impulsiveness of an Anna Karenina.

Sal more than disliked Joe; he hated him. A leech, he called him, because Joe's monthly income from Social Security was even smaller than my mother's meager pensions. He worried that my mother would somehow be hurt by relishing his company through her eighties. "She isn't the same woman we grew up with," he complained; Joe was making her dependent. I saw the same woman, but more relaxed and flexible and sometimes welcoming help with errands or with chores. After a while, Sal stopped visiting my mother's apartment. He'd pick her up and drive her to Jersey to spend a week with him. Then Joe would tell me tales gleaned from my mother about Sal and his third wife. I might have seen their friction as an opening to become the favorite child, but somehow I didn't, just listening on such occasions.

After my mother's surgery and stroke, Sal turned fiercely protective. Like Joe, he traveled two hours each way every day to see her—Joe by two bus lines in Brooklyn, Sal by car from Jersey. Whenever he saw Joe, Sal frowned, and the older man yielded the bedside, bitter and angry at my brother. Sometimes I found Joe alone with my mother; he'd hold her hand, and I saw her straining toward him, wanting to say words she could no longer say. "She's always like that when Joe's here," the nurses told me, "more active and trying."

The last week of her life, my brother found a nursing home for my mother near his suburban home in New Jersey. It made sense, he said—and it did. I live part of the year in North Carolina, and if my mother stayed in Brooklyn, I would not always be able to visit her, even weekly. He could and would visit daily, and the move to Jersey saved him a difficult commute. For him, Joe was not even an issue; on my own, I arranged with Joe that I would rent a car and take him whenever I was in New York. For my mother, the main issue seemed to be staying in a nursing home at all, to which she reacted with agitation.

Two days after the transfer, I got a call from my brother Sal. My mother was running a fever and had an infection. Further surgery might alleviate a block-age and keep her going, but Sal agreed with me now that it would be wrong and against her wishes. It was important for him to believe that my mother no longer understood anything and that her brain was gone—something he said a nurse at the nursing home confirmed. I felt sure as sure could be that she remained alert but trapped within what had become a prison of a body. I felt certain that she was aware, as I was, that even minimal recovery would take many years—and she was in her nineties. I felt her fear of nursing homes, her fate now, and also knew that she wanted to be released, as her hand pressures and blinking eyes had told me more than once. I knew there would be a legacy of guilt, whatever I did or didn't do. But I had drafted and reread her living will and understood what she wanted. I knew her wishes and let it be.

My initial thought when I learned that my brother was dying was that my mother would be so pained and aggrieved that it seemed a blessing she would never know. A terrible cliché, like Mrs. Ramsay in *To the Lighthouse* saying in an unwary moment, "We are in the hands of the Lord." Like her, I drew back and wondered: Why did I say that, even to myself?

My second thought was that I wanted to use the time my brother and I had left as siblings to make time for conversation and space for reconciliation. It felt so strange that, having been so close, I now knew very little about Sal's daily routines, let alone his inner life. I had in mind the possibility of sharing our common memories about the past as a gateway to current emotions: the times we'd made up stories together, and hunted for Christmas presents, and lit fires in the bathroom sink—things I've reconstructed here.

When my husband asked when was the last time I'd had lunch or dinner with my brother alone, just the two of us, I realized that it had been years and years, if ever. I called my brother and arranged to meet for lunch, taking the train to Jersey to meet at the time and place he said would be most convenient and feeling pleased that he was willing to get together. I usually try to avoid making up multiple scenarios, knowing that things often don't work out as planned. But I felt anxious on this occasion and spun out various ways the conversation might go.

As I approached my brother's car, I saw his wife in the passenger seat and, though I like her very much, I knew her presence would make for a different kind of day. Not filled with small talk exactly: They both overflowed with de-tails about his illness and treatments. Patrick Swayze lived, for example, the

longest after his diagnosis of pancreatic cancer, surely exceeded now by Steve
Jobs and Ruth Bader Ginsberg, who had a special, more operable, kind. But
Sal and Lois showed no willingness to talk, as I would have liked, about the
past or the final things we all knew were coming. When lunch ended thirty
minutes before the next train back, they drove me around in their car, with my
brother on his cell phone almost the whole time, taking orders for engineering supplies. I began to suspect what was in fact the case. While my brother
considered me a prime witness to his illness and expected me there, he would
remain closed down emotionally. For decades, I had not known what he did
or felt. And, or so it seemed, I never would. Still, I wanted to be in the picture,
and Sal seemed to want me there.

I traveled back and forth several times from North Carolina, where I was
teaching that term, to visit Sal in the hospital. He always hovered on the brink
of being sent home, and, with him, I went over what needed to happen before
he could leave the hospital, noticing, as he probably did, that each change in
treatment seemed to produce a new problem. My brother dressed as though
each visit was completely routine and at his house. Conversation was general
and almost impersonal. On my next-to-last visit, he was visibly upset to be
undergoing chemo and to be shirtless when I arrived. He fussed and fumed
until he managed to get up and put on his shirt, refusing all offers of help.

A cousin whose beloved wife died of pancreatic cancer shortly after my
mother passed, had alerted me that the endgame comes fast once the patient
loses weight and has abdominal bloating. Since my last visit two weeks ago,
my brother had lost weight and had slight abdominal bloating. But despite
several tries on my part, the conversation remained extremely general. The
only new element—and a real surprise to me—was that my brother had become a devout churchgoer, which he communicated as a simple matter of
fact. He talked a lot about Father Robert, who was becoming a monsignor
and might, my brother feared, be moved to a different parish. I felt a lot of
strain in the room and the sense that certain things must not be said. When
my brother went into the bathroom, my sister-in-law confided physical details
that I knew Sal would not want me to know, and, when he got back into bed,
he repeatedly lost his temper.

His wife had broken down on my previous visit and, as she walked me out,
complained about his moods, saying (they must be common words) that she
"only wants her husband back." (I consider her words a tribute to how many
people feel fairly content with their everyday lives.) This time, a long drama
ensued about her daughter's (my brother's stepdaughter's) arrival with chicken
from Boston Market. The daughter was several hours late. When the yelling
started, I stayed a decent interval longer, then left.

After that, things indeed moved quickly. I called daily, usually reaching Sal. I didn't want to rush the stage when I knew I'd need to call Lois, but all I got was small talk: How were my girls and Stu, what was the weather like in North Carolina, a brief summary of treatments that day. Then, for one whole day and night, I reached only Sal's voicemail. I called his wife early the next morning, and she immediately began crying, suggesting I leave North Carolina before my next planned visit. We had moved from the question of when Sal might go home to whether Sal would be able to be released to a hospice.

I flew back to New York that night and arrived at the hospital early the next day with my husband and daughters to find a brother who looked, astonishingly, very much like my father in the last days of his life. At least twenty years older, in a matter of weeks. It was bad now, and Sal was heavily medicated. His wife pointed out physical details—like blackness on his teeth—as signs of the advancing cancer. Conversations remained all on one side, since, though he could no longer keep up the pretense that he'd be going home, my brother could also no longer respond except by gestures that might be aimless—it was hard to tell. He might have been trying to tell me something meaningful; he might have been telling me to go away; he might not have been aware of me at all. My longest conversations were with his son, distraught and having difficulty coping; he had believed, until just a day or two before, that the problem was the doctor, not the cancer. He showed the same pragmatic attitude that members of my family, maybe all families, use to get through such occasions. What should I call it: repression? shame? taking just one thing at a time? Was he still hoping for a cure or at least a temporary fix? Was it all more mysterious than that? What story or set of stories capture it? What can I give you here? I truly don't know. But, having your own experiences, you may.

My brother died that evening, overnight. When the phone rang at six in the morning, I knew what I'd hear even before I picked up. My nephew made the call. A little later, when I talked with my sister-in-law, she felt devastated that he had died while she had briefly fallen asleep in his room. I reassured her that he might have chosen that moment—conventional enough words and possibly true. Like all "wakes," Sal's had its comic moments as well as its sad ones. I kept thinking that my brother would have laughed with me and our cousins if he could see. But, of course, he couldn't.

A Wheel and a Turn

Now here I need to do a wheel and a turn. The events in my family were sad enough, to be sure, but in the end, I know, quotidian: a father's death, a boy-friend in my mother's life, my brother's anger, her death, my brother's illness, his death. While fictional, the events in Aeschylus refer to epochal, legendary actions: the Trojan War, the death of kings, matricide, the rule of law. Still, let's consider the core elements. A dead father; a mother with a new man; a brother and sister once close, now separate and coming together during matters of life and death, over the mother's situation. Though the play unfolds in a more elevated sphere, the same themes arose in my family.

There's more, hard to unpack and ponder. At some deep level, I felt responsible for my mother's death, for the same reasons that Joe blamed my brother. His beloved Rose looked to her educated children for help when she made her decisions. Despite all our advantages, we made some choices that turned out badly. My father always used to wonder if he had killed his mother, who had pneumonia, when she couldn't breathe and he tried to give her artificial respiration, though he didn't really know how. "Don't think it," my mother would say. Not "you didn't kill her"—but "don't think it." As though—and we all believe this at some level—a possibility doesn't exist if we don't say it out loud.

Great books broach forbidden topics and, as psychology has long acknowledged, enact taboos. They say out loud our worst and most irrational fears and even put them in writing. That's one reason that mythic stories take hold and grip us so, especially at times of loss and change. Reading and rereading great books, finding their patterns in our everyday lives, broadens our experience beyond where we would usually go and reassures us that we're normal. It enriches understanding and allows us to reassess our past. The emotions that govern the *Oresteia* and *Malora* endure and chime with ours: feelings of parents for children, children for parents, siblings and lovers and spouses for each other. There may be stronger things that motivate us—patriotism, altruism, justice, liberty. But familial emotions remain as primary as the urge for survival.

2

Imagining Disaster

Out of Sight

In a scene that disturbs me even now, a murderer tells a woman that she will be his next victim. While she sits transfixed and surprisingly passive, he removes a tie, wraps it around her neck, and begins to strangle her. We do not see the further action—that's part of Alfred Hitchcock's genius as the director of *Frenzy* (1972). Instead, we cut to a dog, closed out of the room and frantically trying to make its way back in. Our attention switches from the victim to the animal, and, to some extent, our sympathy does too. But our imaginations know how to supply the rest.

The oldest trick in the book still works: In art, when something grim and gruesome takes place, it often happens out of sight but not out of mind. Oedipus blinding himself, Jocasta's hanging, Antigone meeting her willful end, Troy's fall in the *Aeneid* and the fate of the hero's wife. Blood, suffering, and death remain all the more vivid when unseen. Stimulated and provoked, the imagination of disaster creates evidence that matches in impact the more graphic violence in, say, a TV show like *Game of Thrones*. Dramatic texts, Aristotle theorized long ago in his *Poetics*, generate catharsis—the pity and fear evoked by tragedy, purged as the work moves swiftly to its end. The residue remains, as it always does, for the survivors, since the dead, as we all know, feel no pain.

More recent great books use similar tricks. In its middle section, "Time Passes," Virginia Woolf's *To the Lighthouse* records as an aside, in brackets, the death of three major characters—Mrs. Ramsay, her daughter Prue, and her son Andrew—all during World War I. When it narrates World War II,

Ian McEwan's *Atonement* performs a similar sleight of hand, killing off two of the major characters but hiding it until near the end.[1] Nabokov's *Lolita* announces its heroine's death in a fake preface, but we do not register it because she is called by her real name (Dolores Schiller), rather than by the name immortalized in the book's title. W. G. Sebald's *Austerlitz* asks us to ponder mass murder through the aura of mute artifacts and aged photographs.[2]

In all such instances, we can't really see what's happening, and yet, in our imaginations, we can't stop looking. My personal history—I'd even say most personal histories—operates that way too. They harbor if not secrets, exactly, then real regrets where we do not dwell.

Second Opinions

If great books and our life histories form living tissue, it's important not to strain or tear the flesh. So, I've been hesitant to write what I'm about to write. There are facts in my personal history from which I've taught myself to look away, not wanting to live in the constant memory of disaster. It's denial, New York Italian-American style—not pathological but not necessarily healthy either.

Though people tend to forget, because it's painful, I lost my only son, my first child, in infancy. He was born with a heart defect we were told could be corrected by surgery at the proper time. I cherished every ounce of his baby flesh, always startled, and a little worried, by the uncanny depth of wisdom in his eyes. There were many crises in his short life, but the most important came when he failed to gain weight after three months and was switched to solid food in an attempt to help. "Growth arrest," the doctor called it. I'd been nursing him, so his failure to grow felt deeply personal.

A sweet-tempered baby, he ate eagerly the mashed banana and cereal we offered. Then, suddenly, he experienced an accelerated, far too rapid heartbeat. As the doctors advised, we waited fifteen minutes and then took his pulse again. Swallowing panic, thirty minutes later, the same thing. Then, as the doctors prescribed, we rushed from rural western Massachusetts, where we lived, to Boston, and faced a terrible choice that only we could make.

The doctors said we could authorize surgery immediately and probably have a healthy child. It was always *probably*; the way they put it was that the boy would never be an athlete but would be healthy. Or we could delay and quite possibly precipitate brain damage. The doctors strongly recommended immediate surgery—even though, just days before, they'd wanted to wait a year to diminish the risk of doing complex heart surgery on a tiny baby.

As I write, I am processing fully only now, some thirty years later, that we were given a treacherous Sophie's kind of choice. Take the better odds for survival in surgery at age one but quite possibly have a brain-damaged child. Or operate now, putting life itself at greater risk for a chance at almost complete normality.

The nurse-practitioner assigned to our case once said that people get the burdens they can bear. I don't like such homilies and didn't then, but I found a core of truth in this one. We had learned during the three months of Matthew's life that we could bear having a child with a heart defect; we didn't need an athlete or crave physical perfection. We couldn't bear having a child with brain damage we'd caused by our inaction. The surgery, we were told, had to be done the very next morning and had an excellent chance for success, just 2 to 5 percent less than waiting a full year. Having been in top percentages in other categories, we didn't like the odds. But when we asked to get a second opinion, we were told that, because July 4 was just two days away, getting one would delay the surgery until July 6, and by then brain damage might well have happened. My husband and I went to eat and talk and make a decision.

We both favored surgery, which made things easier than a split opinion would have been. Then my husband said, wisely I think—though it also had consequences for us both, but perhaps especially for me—"Marianna. And if we make this decision to operate, we can't look back. If it goes wrong, it will tear us to pieces if we do." (As I write those words, and even as I reread them, I can hear his voice, and tears spring to my eyes.) I agreed. We made the decision.

As we sat and waited four long hours for the surgery to end—too long, we both knew—the music in the waiting room was (I will never forget this), "May the Circle Be Unbroken." I was rereading *War and Peace* and getting to the section where the little princess, Prince Andrei's first wife, dies. It seemed like a bad omen. I wanted to stop reading, but I already knew what came next.

Our baby died in heart surgery.

Afterward, the doctors sounded shocked when they told us that his aorta had been too narrow to sustain life, so that waiting the extra months would not have mattered. His condition had been fatal from birth, and it was highly unusual and contrary to medical norms that he had survived even three months. They sounded genuinely surprised and interested in the way that doctors do in special cases. I imagined, though I censored the thought, that they'd had to make a decision in the operating room on whether to abort the surgery and let the baby live as long as possible or whether to end it there—though, of course, I do not know. A few weeks later, when I had confirmed with research and a doctor friend what they said about a narrow aorta, I called the hospital to speak once more to the surgeon. It troubled me in ways I found hard to define when I learned he was no longer there. Was there any connection to Matthew's death?

We were shown Matthew's corpse in a storage room and told the nurse to await funeral arrangements from us. We had had a three-month-old infant, not a stillbirth, and did not, as she suggested, want the hospital to "handle it."

Until I wrote these words, I thought that my mother's corpse was the first I'd seen. But my son was the first dead body, outside of a funeral home. "It's good for her to see them," my father would always say, about funerals and corpses. Matter without spirit. As preparation. Though it's no preparation at all.

As we drove home from Boston, we were so distraught that we entered the thruway in the wrong direction but stopped before it was too late. It was a wake-up call, like one I'd have much later when I drove miles on a flat tire, generating smoke. But it was not yet, as it would be then, even remotely time to begin to move on. We reversed direction, pulled over, and cried it out until we felt ready to make the drive.

I did get a second opinion when my mother fell ill, though I sometimes think I failed to follow through. The consultation came by phone and the doctor, who had a strong Indian accent, told me in no uncertain terms that if my mother did not elect surgery quite soon to remove the tumor located in a key position of her colon, she would die later in excruciating pain or quickly bleed out. I am trying now to remember the position of the tumor: high on the descending colon, I think. I was too panicked when I spoke to him to recall or even to put pen to paper.

My mother was in her nineties. Perhaps letting her die over a year or two would have been the better choice than precipitating the stroke that left her in the hospital and liable to the infection that killed her more quickly. But, of course, we couldn't know that until it was too late. I reacted to the horror in the doctor's voice, recoiled, and, along with my brother, recommended the surgery to my Mom—who did, after all, make the final choice.

I might have stopped everything again in the hospital. After a diagnostic minor operation before the cancer surgery, my mother told me that, if they found cancer in the tissue samples they took, she would not be willing to have chemotherapy. She had seen my father and some friends have chemo, so I understood and respected her decision. I also knew, as she did, that unless she were extremely lucky and the cancer fully contained, the doctors would almost surely recommend chemo.

At that point, there are several things I might have said. "Let's wait," for example. "Go home, recover a bit, think about it, and then have the major operation if you wish." That's what her consort, Joe, strongly wanted—for her to have the chance to regain her strength. Like the doctors, my brother was emphatic that he wanted the operation done as soon as possible. Suggesting that my mother wait would have meant displeasing my brother and siding with Joe.

Even though I am an educated, strong-minded woman, somehow it seemed too late to buck the doctors and my brother. I told myself that the samples *might* come back cancer-free or that Mom might change her mind about the chemo. There was no time for me to confirm the odds except by consulting her doctor, who had already given us his opinion that surgery was highly likely to succeed—whatever that meant to him. After the minor procedure, my mother had recovered quickly from anesthesia, a major danger to elderly people who'd never had it and a major fear when old people go under. When my mother decided that the cancer surgery was a risk worth taking, I agreed and even felt proud of her for being confident.

My passivity during these moments is bad. It's really, really bad. But there was another factor in the background—a nagging, terrible, small detail that became significant.

For many months, I had a keynote address scheduled in Europe, in Bologna, the week the doctors planned the surgery. It would, in fact, have been more convenient for me to give my mother a few weeks to wait and recover from the first, minor, procedure before deciding to do the more major operation. I could have gone to Bologna and returned easily by then. It would have been more convenient for me to back my mother's partner Joe, who couldn't see the wisdom of doing everything at once and taxing an elderly woman's body. But the doctors and my brother were adamant: the doctors because they had stopped administering Cumadin, a blood-thinning medication, and were concerned about a stroke; my brother for that reason but also because he'd found it burdensome to check her into the hospital and because he feared that, if she went home, Joe would convince her not to risk the cancer surgery at all.

Oddly enough, my having a major lecture to give made me want to avoid intervening in a way that might be self-serving. I have read George Eliot and Henry James, and, much as I admire those authors, they favor self-abnegation and self-sacrifice in ways damaging in ordinary life. My mother agreed to do the full surgery on this hospitalization. I supported and even applauded her decision. She went for the operation, joking with the doctors while I waited with her for it to begin.

It's already shameful that I mentally consulted Henry James and George Eliot, even briefly, on this occasion. Really, I should have known better and acted selfishly, as their characters do not. I should, at least, have slowed down the hospital's machinery, since I knew enough by this point in my life not to trust absolutely what doctors say. It was, as I say, really bad already. But we have not yet come to the part I truly regret.

My mother's surgery was scheduled for early on the same day that I was supposed to fly to Bologna on a very late overnight flight. My ticket had been purchased months before and could not be changed. It would mess up the conference if I did not come on schedule, though I had sent my lecture by e-mail ahead of me, just in case someone else needed to deliver it. My mother was having major surgery, so I decided to make a fate-bet, Italian-American style. I'd pack my bag and bring it with me to the hospital. But I would take the plane only if the surgery went well *and* I got to talk to the doctor *and* I got to see my mother in recovery *and* my brother, husband, and Joe would all be on the scene overnight. All these things happened, though they easily might not have. I talked to my mother in recovery and held her hand.

Her eyes were rolling wildly, I imagined because the pain of major surgery surprised her, even under drugs. She squeezed my hand and seemed responsive when I said I would be back in just three days. We had talked in advance about the possible trip, and she had seen no reason why I shouldn't go. My brother and his wife were at the hospital, and they would both stay overnight. My husband would be there too, as would Joe. I would be back in three short days. Euphoric that she had come through, with a good report from the doctors, I felt it might be less than optimistic to stay. I got on the plane and arrived ten hours later in Bologna.

When I checked into my hotel, I got a message to call my husband in New York no matter what the time. I knew it had to be a crisis; my hands fumbled at the numbers as I placed the call. The day after surgery, my mother had suffered a major stroke. The good news was that she'd been in a hospital that specializes in strokes, and they had operated again and saved her. Another facility might not have been able to do so. The bad news was that they could not assess the damage to her brain just yet, but there had been enough to cause loss of speech and paralysis on one side, at least for the time being. I tried to fly back immediately, but the airline had no seats. The next morning, Italian time, my brother calmly pointed out by phone that I might be needed for weeks, months, or even years in our new situation. I should stay where I was, do my lecture, and then fly home as planned. It sounded right.

I had a miserable time at the conference. Averse to small talk, I took a train by myself to Venice, where I'd taught just months before my mother's fatal illness. I wanted simply to ride the vaporetto both ways to and from San Marco at sunset, just to think. As if I were a first-time tourist, my heart yearned toward buildings I'd passed every day when I lived there. Except that, unlike the tourists, I did not want to remember the occasion and took no photos.

When I got back to New York, I learned that, though there might be some improvement within the week, my mother was still paralyzed on one side and could not speak. In my absence, my brother had authorized a feeding tube, which I knew would be against my mother's wishes. I had drafted her living will and might not have agreed had I been present. But I had not been present. It was done, and, legally, nothing could be changed.

I have called my mother and my brother "stoic," and I have some of that quality too, which favors inaction and reacts to grief internally. I have already told you that the story ends with my mother's death a few weeks later. Would it have been better to let her die more gradually from the colon cancer, as would surely have happened? Might the cancer have grown slowly enough for her to die of some other cause? Would she have grown bitter over the unusual lack of energy she'd felt recently, which would only have gotten worse? Would that bitterness have marred her life even more than the last few weeks did? We'll never know. None of us.

In Ian McEwan's *Atonement*, when faced with unforgiveable things she has done, the character Briony chooses to write fiction that gives beloved people she's betrayed long, happy lives. "In a story, you only had to wish, you only had to write it down and you could have the world," she writes. It reminds me of what I've called the oldest trick in the book: in art, having death and destruction occur out of sight; in life, repressing and denying what seems too painful to recall.

The story you are reading is neither play nor fiction. We make decisions that turn out badly, decisions we don't like, decisions we would make differently a second time. Violence occurs in front of us or out of sight—but, either way, it's devastation. We can't just write it down and save the world.

3

Mother's Day

This chapter talks a lot, even quite a lot, about yoga, meditation, and the memory of my mother. It's also really personal. If the yoga, the meditation, or the intense personal quality bothers you, please feel free to skip to the next chapter, grounded in Homer's *Odyssey* and Tolstoy's *War and Peace*. I need to say upfront that the chapter may raise the hackles of people who think of yoga as cultural appropriation. But I believe, quite firmly, that yoga and meditation are gifts from South Asia *meant to be given* that now form part of American culture too. We may disagree on that, but there it is: I do yoga and practice meditation as an American who usually lives in the hurly-burly, frenetic rhythm of New York. So, sorry.

After my mother died, alongside many Western great books, I read a host of yoga classics, a veritable who's who: Pantanjali's *Sutras*, *The Life of Ramakrishna*, Steven Cope's *Yoga and the Search for the True Self*, B. K. S. Iyengar's *Light on Yoga*, Mark Whitwell's *Yoga of Heart: The Healing Power of Intimate Connection*, Sandra Gilbert's *Eat, Pray, Love*, and more—a mix of the ancient and the modern, the profound and the fluffy. Inspired by my readings, I decided to tune up my physical yoga practice, even toying with the idea of undertaking a year of teacher training.

But with short arms, a weak core, knees that protrude inward, and what I call foundational thighs, I am and always have been much happier with breath control and meditation than with the poses that make up physical yoga. I knew that doing so much of what's called hatha yoga would be challenging, but I took a lot of workshops anyway. Gradually, as I began facing grief, I reduced the physical side of yoga and amped up the meditation aspect, for which Patanjali's *Sutras* are central, classic texts.

"Now begins the study of yoga," the ancient yoga *Sutras* say, an opening that gets translated from the original Sanskrit in multiple ways. Some emphasize the giving of knowledge by others to a relatively passive "you," others, the receiving of ancient wisdom by someone ready to spring into action:

Now, the teachings of yoga;
Now the exposition of Yoga is being made;
Now, after previous preparation, begins yoga.

All versions emphasize that you have to be "in the moment," as common parlance puts it: to *Be Here Now,* according to the title of a wildly popular 1971 book by the American teacher Richard Alpert, also known as Baba Ram Dass. Called "the seer" and "the self" in the next lines of the *Sutras,* the student begins by restraining the mind from exploring the sensory world and abiding "in its own nature." As Swami Sachidananda, a founder of Integral Yoga, puts it, "You are not the body nor the mind," but "the mind must be quiet; otherwise it seems to distort the truth."[1]

Many gurus gloss the *sutras,* a word that means *verses, aphorisms,* or *sayings,* written down by Pantanjali, a mythic figure about whom not much is known.[2] What we do know is that Pantanjali lived sometime between 200 BC and 400 CE and that his legend includes many mythic patterns that appear in the stories of other holy men, including virgin birth.

Fortunately for me, who will never be physically adept, the *sutras* designate various methods beyond physical postures to quiet the mind. One can concentrate on breath, slowing it down as much as possible; one can contemplate an image, for example, the face of a valued teacher; one can use a chant or mantra. Anything that is "elevating" can lead to *samadhi,* the pure white light of eternity, a blissful state that only comes when "the memory is well purified" (Swami Sachidananda again). In places like New York, the state of samadhi has to be put aside before reentering the streets and subways; to some extent, the same is true even within ashrams devoted to meditation, since certain household tasks must be done. The state of samadhi is thus never constant but something that must be recreated daily. I worked hard at recreating it daily.

But despite all this yoga and meditation, I continued to feel pissy at home and sniped often at my husband, endangering the core relationship of my daily life. Contrary to Mark Whitwell's title, after my mother died, yoga of the heart was not happening for me. Since I was on leave from teaching, traveling and a change of scene seemed like good options—and I took them. With my yoga books and classics of literature packed side by side, I undertook, quite deliberately, some mid-to-late-life journeys, including six weeks in Santa Fe that ended shortly after Mother's Day. My trip to Santa Fe begins with a woe linked, like everything else at this point in my life, to my mother.

Inflamed

As I packed for New Mexico and shuttled through two airports, I developed a rousing case of sciatica—an inflammation of the largest nerve in the body. Running across the sacrum, wrapping around each hip, and extending down each leg, irritation of the sciatic nerve can show up as pain in the lower back, soreness in the hip, or (the worst!) shooting pains down the leg. As anyone who has had sciatica can testify, the injury can be pure misery. As any good yogi will tell you, sciatica blocks and inflames the root of life.

My first bout of sciatica occurred perhaps thirty-five years ago when, bent over and using a hand roller, I spent an unhappy day waterproofing a deck. Sciatica can be a domestic woe, associated with that kind of chore, or—and this makes sense—it can also arise in connection with the opposite stress of leaving home. Shortly after this first attack, I decided to try yoga, a practice I had followed but then abandoned when I moved from Massachusetts to North Carolina. I got lucky.

"Inhale. Exhale. The breath is the main thing in yoga, and you've got to time it along with the movements and flows": My teacher, a woman a decade older than I am, was starting up a group. Her high-pitched, nasal voice—pure New York or New Jersey—drove some people crazy, and they quickly left the class. But that touch of Brooklyn didn't bother me. This woman, whom I'll call Joyce, saw herself as initiating into yoga people who either had never done it or done it so long ago that it scarcely counted—my own situation. She began slowly, which was just what I needed. In fact, for perhaps six months, my greatest joy in yoga was what's called *savasana*, corpse pose, done lying down on the back, a state of total relaxation and surrender used routinely at the end of class. I didn't know it then, but even in my zeal for savasana I was well on my way to becoming a committed yogi, despite the many ways that my body differs from those on the cover of *Yoga Journal*.

After doing yoga for years with Joyce, I thought sciatica was a thing of the past, something I would never experience again. And, in fact, it didn't return for more than five years. But, like most nerve injuries, sciatica can recur. After my mother died, I got it bad when I went to Santa Fe.

I arrived in Santa Fe on Easter Sunday. That date, which would have significance for anyone, had extra significance for me. By chance, Easter Sunday fell that year on April 16, my mother's birthday and also—a perfect confluence of cosmic coincidences—my brother's birthday and the birthday of Joe, my mother's late-life partner. My first child, Matthew, was born on April 21, one day after my father's birthday and close to the birthday of Stanley, a friend and colleague who has influenced some of my life's sharpest changes. April 20 is also Adolf Hitler's birthday, something my father used to mention with amusement, although it concerned me when I was close to giving birth to Matthew. If dates have fateful energy, April 16 does for me. This April 16 had special meaning. My mother died on December 15, four months and a day earlier. April 16 would have been her ninety-first birthday.

As I drove into Santa Fe on the sixteenth, or, rather, as my husband did (usual for us on longer hauls), I had a peculiar and even spooky sense of my mother's presence, more so than I'd had since her death. I know that may sound strange, but it's true, and part of this story. Given it was her birthday, it even makes sense, emotionally. Later that day, in a café, I was looking at a ring I wear all the time, which reset the stones of my mother's engagement ring. Since I never take it off, I hadn't really noticed it in years. Then a stone caught the light, and my mother's face was there, simply there. Not a ghost or a vision. But a presence, like something in a Toni Morrison novel.

That first day in Santa Fe, my sciatica raged, and I knew there would be no yoga for me. Perhaps, I thought, it was just as well. I'd been doing yoga daily in New York and North Carolina and could do other things while here. But one thing I would not skip, sciatica or not, was meditation. "Every day you brush your teeth," my New York teacher says. "Without it, your teeth feel crummy—all coated and clogged. Your mind is like that too. You should no more skip a day of meditation than skip a day of brushing your teeth."

So, I brush my mental teeth.

Because I wanted to be able to walk and bike in Santa Fe, I needed to heal quickly, and so, for the first time ever, I perched on a rigid chair rather than sit on the floor, which might aggravate the injury. I closed my eyes, and my husband joined me. He'd left some jazz, Miles Davis, playing in the background. I would rather have had some chants or nature music and had been prone, recently, to feel annoyed at him. But I had begun a simple smile meditation and let it go.

With a gentle "Buddha" smile on my face, I imagined it traveling throughout my body, relaxing every limb and soothing every inner organ. When her teacher tells her to smile into her liver in *Eat, Pray, Love*, Elizabeth Gilbert accurately describes the smile meditation. A liver will do as a marker. So will the colon or a kidney. Did the smile meditation work? Well . . . yes and no. I felt better afterward, but not perfect. Something physical and not just psychological had caused my sciatica, and the body would heal slowly. Still, the meditation had helped.

The second day, my sciatica was in what I'd call full bloom, more localized but also more intense. Overnight, I had become aware that lifting my rib cage off my hips eased the pressure and that the pain responded well to a soothing motion of stroking downward. It occurred to me that, when yoga teachers encouraged me to reach up with my arms, hands linked, arms straight, as high as I can, they might have been—make that probably *were*—telling me to lift my ribs as far from my hips as I can. I began to suspect, as I did several more times in Santa Fe, that my sciatica came from compression around my hips, a.k.a. slumping, which became worse after my mother died.

I put both of these discoveries to use by doing a second smile meditation that segued spontaneously to what's called a *sut yam* (the first vowel is short, with an "au" sound) meditation, a technique for dealing with pain—psychological pain—but why not, I thought, physical pain too.

Again, the technique is simple and depends upon willing visualization.

Sitting tall in a meditation posture, I once again sat in a chair, though the floor would have been better, and did rapid breaths in and out through my nose (called *bhastrika*, or "skull shining" breath). These stir up the bottom two chakras, yoga talk for energy centers or clusters of nerves in the body, in this case the perineum and the region just below the navel. Done sincerely and with surrender, *bhastrika* makes yogis feel the effects of energy movement in some form (usually heat) as it rises first to the navel, then to the chest, and finally to the top of the head. Meditation requires a lot of what Coleridge called "suspension of disbelief" and a fair amount of imagination.

Then—and this is the core of the *sut yam* technique—one releases the pain through the crown, which of course can't really happen except in the imagination. Chanting *sut yam*, silently, one allows (read, imagines) the sensation of pain releasing out through the opening of what once was the fontanel. Though it's no silver bullet, the technique produces a sensation of what Renato Rosaldo calls "lightening," the feeling the Ilongot we met in the Introduction get from collecting heads.

After I performed the technique and came out of meditation, I felt better. Then I remembered something important and dramatic that I had apparently put out of mind. The last time I used the *sut yam* technique was when I held my mother's hand at her deathbed and chanted not for me, but for her, as she moved closer to death.

After three weeks of looking angry after her postsurgery stroke, my mother's face had become extraordinarily peaceful. It seemed as if she was glad the time had come to let her go—something my brother had been reluctant to accept until this very day, something I promised her I would do as soon as it was clear she would not recover and we could release her from the hospital's ever-vigilant desire to perform just one more procedure that would move us past the current problem to arrive, as we learned, at the next.

It was snowing that day, with accumulations rising, when my brother called. He told me that I should come to the hospice in southern Jersey where he had just transferred my mother but that he'd understand if I couldn't. He didn't want to leave her side and could not pick me up at the train as usual. I felt irrationally panicky about how to get there and irrationally panicky about not going. These were the times before Uber, or the answer would have seemed obvious. It did seem obvious to my husband: We should rent a car, and he would drive. While he arranged that, I quickly dressed and decided not to delay leaving in order to contact and pick up my daughters, who would be at work. In retrospect, that seems a dubious choice. But my brother and I, my nephew, and all our spouses would be there, so at the time it seemed all right.

My mother's breath was slow when we arrived. Her face, as smooth at ninety as a fifty-year-old's, looked tranquil. Her hands, far younger looking than my own, responded to mine with pressure at the appropriate moments, so that I believed that she could, as the nurses told us, still understand what we were saying even though, under morphine, she could feel no pain.

With a tenderness unusual for him, my brother instructed me, as the hospice nurses had instructed him, to tell my mother that we were there, that we loved her, and that we would take care of everything. It was all right to leave now, it was okay to go. After about two hours, her breathing slowed substantially. At this point, I repeated *sut yam* until I felt her spirit depart—a cliché that is only too true.

My mother's passing was so quiet that we had to confirm her death with a nurse and doctor, who responded quickly. But, of course, I knew, just as I knew when to tell my brother to hold my mother's other hand about half an hour before she died. Afterward, without saying anything to one another, my family drifted into another room to talk.

Now, in Santa Fe, almost five months later and still facing grief, as I came out of the meditation, I reexperienced the entire sequence of my mother's death for the first time. I felt shaken but also, to borrow Renato Rosaldo's term one more time, "lighter." Having revisited painful moments I'd been avoiding, I also felt open to what the remainder of my stay might bring.

Cores

In Santa Fe, the "City Different," as it calls itself, almost everyone seems, paradoxically, like me: lefty, health conscious, into yoga, and (more often than I'd like to admit) either my daughters' age (roughly one-third of the downtown population) or my age and older. It's the kind of place where, walking into a coffee shop, you see non-Asians wearing kundalini yoga garb: white shirts and pants with white Sikh turbans. A culture-appropriator-phobe's nightmare.

Though my husband and I found a kundalini place we liked a lot, most of the yoga we did was at a studio that billed itself as Ashtanga and Iyengar — posture- and alignment-based schools we usually avoid because their guiding principle is the mastery of poses. The Iyengar website features photos of its founder B. K. S. Iyengar in a series of postures that I will never do as well as he does and, in many cases, will never do at all. I usually shy away from Iyengar-based classes because they include so many portions I want to skip, sometimes without offering the invitation to adapt the practice to my body or even just to rest, if that's what I want to do.

Once my sciatica eased, I tried what's called Restorative Yoga at this Iyengar place — basically, resting in poses supported by pillows — and the studio turned out to be less rigid than I expected. A thoughtful teacher modified each pose in great detail to meet the needs of my still-sore body. "Move one step at a time," she said. "Put down your hands and test how it feels. Then shift your body slowly." It was so simple but just what I needed. Move slowly. Reflect. Adjust. Then move some more. The simple phrases seemed like symbolic metaphors for facing grief. Move slowly. Reflect. Adjust. Then move some more. Within a week, I felt ready for more strenuous physical yoga. Only now did I recognize the fly in the Iyengar ointment.

One night, we took a class called "Asanas and Pranayama" — poses and breathing — as a stepping stone to more physically demanding work. The class turned out to be pretty much what I would call restorative, with a lot of time on our backs, in poses that riff off savasana (corpse pose). The teacher said that some of the poses were designed to access the back part of the brain and to release deep emotions — again, please, take that as you will, skeptically or not.

Trained by now in meditation, and flat on my back, midway through the class my mind moved deeply into meditative states, even though one normally meditates sitting upright. After a while, I felt puzzled. The teacher kept moving us in and out of physical positions, some of them rather elaborate. But she did not take any steps to bring us back gradually from deep meditation into an awareness of the body before doing so, something good teachers, like this one, should do.

When I asked her afterward whether the class had been an alternative to typical meditations, she looked at me with incomprehension. The class, she insisted, had not involved meditation at all. It was a pre-meditation class and even a pre-yoga class. What's more — I could see it on her face and hear it in her voice — she was appalled that the likes of me, barely out of restorative and unable to do wheel or headstand, would even *think* of meditating. When I replied that I'd worked in different traditions and had meditated on and off for years, now daily for eighteen minutes, she smiled in a way I had trouble processing until I remembered.

She's Iyengar trained. And as B. K. S. Iyengar says, "It is through the alignment of the body that I discovered the alignment of my mind, self, and intelligence."[3] First things first, according to Iyengar: the body and, only then, breathing and meditation. This teacher was one of the purest Iyengar teachers at the studio, and according to her, a student needs to graduate from mastering *all* the asanas to mastering pranayama (breath control) and only then to meditate for extended periods. She believed that I shouldn't meditate until I had been doing physical yoga for at least two years and had perfected it. I knew that, though I have practiced physical yoga for far more than two years, I will never perfect it. For her, I had skipped some steps by doing breath control and meditation *before* Iyengar says my body should; my body, this teacher would say, was not ready for meditation. I say, fiddlesticks. In short, the teacher thought I was an idiot and wasn't sure how to disillusion me. Hence the cryptic smile.

I decided to seek out other teachers at the studio who led classes that could be freely adapted. Two weeks later, I took a class with a lovely, unpretentious woman who immediately set the class at ease. Come savasana, I was stretched on the floor and felt content. It was a deep savasana, in which the teacher said to relax the mouth and surrender the jaw. As I did, I suddenly felt *inside my mother's body at the moment of her passing*, when her face, already relaxed, surrendered, becoming over the next thirty minutes or so a black hole. The sensation connected with how I had relived the hour of her death when I chanted *sut yam* but went several steps further.

A flood of sadness washed over me. I couldn't tell if my mother had been sad (I rather suspect not; she had been ready). But I could tell that I was sad and that sadness and acquaintance with death were real factors in my life right now, however much I traveled and paid attention to other things. Tears seeped from the corners of my eyes—something not unprecedented during savasana or meditation but extremely rare for me. I was in public and not the kind of person who wants to be seen in tears, so I patched up my face as best I could and headed to breakfast, which I knew would do me good. Still, I took from this session the awareness of sadness in my heart. Not always surfacing and certainly not my only feeling all the time. But there.

The following week—and this is the last yoga experience I will revisit here—I opted for what I thought would be a less intense experience at a Mother's Day class billed as "gentle." The teacher ended the class by reading a poem narrated from the point of view of a Vietnamese mother so disoriented by the war that she does not know who's winning. The poem asked the woman a series of questions: the year, the month, the time of day, whether her village still survives, what she believes. In answer to all these questions, the poem's refrain was always "I don't know." In the last stanza, the narrator asked the woman, "Are these your children?" and the ear, primed by the refrain, expected "I don't know." Instead, the answer came back, "Yes."

Prone in savasana, the line hit me in the gut, and I began to cry. Then, when I got up, I saw a couple, both brunettes and maybe in their late thirties, still sitting and meditating while everyone else dispersed. Suddenly, the woman put her face in her hands, her shoulders shaking, while the man comforted her. I didn't need to ask. It was my first Mother's Day without my mother too.

My tears may have primed the pump. For all at once, or so it seemed, I opened to the core issues that were producing my symptoms of sciatica, core issues triggered by my mother's death that had produced a sense of crisis.

What did it mean to be in a place like Santa Fe and to experience strain where the heart has rested for decades? It meant a lot, since there was not a great deal to do in Santa Fe besides yoga, particularly for people who had been there before and especially for someone like me on this trip, warily nursing an injury that placed hiking and biking out of bounds.

The crux of the issue, the reason it felt like a crisis, came from the ease with which I use the pronoun "us," not "me"—a core sense that I am and have been for a very long time part of a couple. Not a perfect couple, to be sure, not even an entirely likely couple—but what couple, I've always thought, really is? But a couple that shares basic values (in fact, we have never disagreed on major decisions), traveled around the world, sustained sexual attraction, and have together lost a first child, endured a miscarriage, experienced the death of all four parents, and raised two beloved daughters. There was, and is, a lot of glue in the relationship.

But in Santa Fe, we had had a lot of arguments, quite a lot of arguments, ones typical of those since my mother's death. What I perceived as his slackness met what he perceived as my critical coldness, and we were off and running. Stu and I love to eat out and (in normal, not COVID times) usually have one meal at a restaurant most days. Generally, eating out and conversation go together easily, but not on this trip. In the past, we'd made fun of couples who sit glumly opposite each other or actively quarrel or spend the entire meal looking at their cell phones. But at least three times in Santa Fe, we had such a bad time at dinner that both of us felt wary. This fairly new and unpleasant pattern unrolled during a period when meditation and self-study were major items on both our agendas. It seemed paradoxical and unfortunate, but there it was.

After that unusual yoga class in savasana, when we were invited to go into our "back brains," Stu said he'd had the worst headache he'd ever had—rare for him, who almost never has headaches. My husband is more volatile and emotional than I am and comes from a loving family but also, by my family's standards, an odd one. He is ten years younger than his adored sister, whose politics swing right, and seven years younger than his brother, who died young (a likely suicide) and was smart, angry, and, I suspect, verbally abusive. That evening, I had brushed off Stu's comments, but now, after my opening experience on Mother's Day, I felt more able to put myself in his place and to understand that when I seem testy, he overreacts because it hurts him; that, in turn, hurts me.

So, the next time an argument got ready to happen—over something too petty to be worth mentioning—I decided to try something different. Stu made a remark that I could meet aggressively, which would trigger my coldness and the cycle we both hate. So instead of answering anything at all, I smiled. He smiled back. Then he told me about an experience he had the night before, when he relaxed and tried to sleep but felt his inner body moving at a hundred miles an hour, refusing to stay still. Core experiences were, clearly, happening for both of us in Santa Fe.

I realized at the time that there was a connection, surely, to my mother's death. But the connection remained obscure until I wrote this piece and remembered a story my mother's boyfriend told me.

"Ten-a years. Ten-a wonderful years. She was so happy!" my mother's boyfriend Joe said repeatedly after she died, sincerely but so often that it seemed almost by rote. Eighty-four to her ninety (a younger man!), with a shock of thick white hair, ruddy skin, and large, thick glasses that magnified his eyes, Joe made my mother's loss more palpable and painful for me in all kinds of ways. He was used to being with her every day, as I was not. He felt that the best part of his life was behind him when she died and that the rest would be anticlimactic at best; I, by contrast, was trying hard to move into the future. Until his own death, about eight years after my mother's, an aging Joe maintained a small shrine to my mother in his room and took two separate bus lines to visit her grave on her birthday and on the anniversary of her death to leave bouquets: "Roses for my Rosa," he'd say. A true romantic.

"Why didn't we meet each other when we were young?" Joe told me my mother asked him—a remark he repeated to me several times over the years and one that still gives me pause. My parents were a happy couple—so it's a question I can't seem to forget and one, I suspect, that made me question my own marriage after my mother's death in a way that, in retrospect, seems natural: major turning points requiring reaffirmation.

Did my mother really, often and vigorously, and not just near the start of her relationship with Joe, think about an alternative life? A life that would not have included me? Did she really want the past undone and value most her late-life new beginning? Without waiting for my response, which—like any child and, for that matter, like any adult—I still have trouble formulating, Joe spared me one. He shrugged in the fatalistic Italian way I'd seen again and again at my mother's funeral, when the most frequent words uttered by far were, "What are you gonna do?"

In his heavily accented English, and like the pragmatic man he was, Joe said, "And I told-a her. What are you gonna do? How could we meet? Me in I-ta-lie? And you in A-mer-i-ca?"

PART II

Sustaining Things

4

Second Chances

How Not to Read the Classics

The thin, nervous-looking young man chain-smoked. As a long ash gathered at the tip of his cigarette, it dangled, rarely falling.[1] The cigarette hung from a thin hand, held in a pose like an imitation of Fred Astaire, the man's legs crossed, his hands shifting rapidly between the cigarette, his disheveled brown hair, and a book. The man wore a rumpled gray suit and a white shirt with a thin tie or, occasionally, a bow tie, intended to be jaunty. When he lit one of his cigarettes, sometimes before extinguishing the last, or when he picked up a book to read a passage, his hands shook. My first exposure to the *Odyssey* with this teacher turned out to be a lesson in how not to read the classics.

I was sixteen and a freshman in college—young, but not all that unusual in New York—and taking a required course. The *Odyssey* might have seemed juicy—as it had for centuries and would soon enough for me. But the teacher gave entirely perfunctory lectures and built the course around weekly quizzes that asked students to identify quotations not by theme or importance but by the book and episode in which they appear—miserable stuff and a waste of spirit. Italo Calvino says that "we do not read the classics out of duty or respect, but only out of love. Except at school." I was "at school" and the teacher, fulfilling his duty.[2] I realize now but did not then that the teacher was probably a thirty-something graduate student less concerned with teaching or even reading than with finishing his dissertation.

Twelve years later, I was a college professor and a new mother, with an infant in my arms as I read the *Odyssey* in snatches, the book I'd chosen for when the baby dozed after nursing. He was still at the stage I call "babies from outer space," a wonderful warm alien inches away whose eyes and face looked but did not really lock on mine. He was my first child and had a heart defect of great and even overwhelming concern to me. In retrospect, it seems possible that I chose the *Odyssey* unconsciously for the same reasons I turned to it after my mother died. It's a touch-base book, a story about wives, husbands, mothers, fathers, sons, society, and how to govern: subjects that, if we add "daughters" to that list, continue to matter most.[3] The memory of why I chose it goes too far back for me to recall—and I don't want to fake a reason. I was in distress but carrying on and hoping that we, this baby and I, would have a long history in which Matthew's need for major surgery would become a smaller and smaller part.

I remember quite strongly how the reading seemed like a revelation. Suddenly, I loved this book, which is all about family, the messiness of change, and the need to find your way back home. Within the next few years, I taught courses in the classics, reading and teaching Dante with students in a special winter session at Williams College and then, the following year, *War and Peace*. Later, at Duke University, I taught a course on epics that included Homer, Dante, and Tolstoy along with Vergil, Milton, and Faulkner. The classics, at the right time, open themselves up and open *us* up.

Fully grown now and the mother of adult daughters, I picked up the *Odyssey* after my mother died with anticipation and the kind of high hopes with which you go to see a play that's gotten rave reviews or a movie nominated for Best Picture. The *Odyssey* was the third or fourth classic I reread after my mother died, a lag time I think now was deliberate because I associated it with my first child's death. On this reading, now fully aware of grief and the need for mourning, I found a glitch. I still loved the *Odyssey*, but there were things I really didn't like. Not at all. No longer a student and not in school, I felt entitled to say so.

I winced when I reread the slaughter of the suitors at the end of the *Odyssey*, over which Telemachus and his father truly bond. Odysseus has been secretive about his homecoming to Ithaca: It's prudent but also sneaky. I love how, in a recent book, Daniel Mendelsohn's father saw right through the pieties that surround Odysseus as a character.[4] Older now, on this reading, I saw through them too. Our hero coldly plans mass slaughter in scenes that later influenced Mario Puzo when he wrote *The Godfather*, a novel and a film I have often taught that riffs on the ten-year timespan and on the structure of Homer's work.

As I neared the end, I approached reluctantly words I remembered from my college years when Odysseus hangs the household maids who had slept with his enemies: "So that all might die a pitiful, ghastly death . . . they kicked up their heels for a little—not for long" (22:498–99).[5] As Margaret Atwood puts it in the preface to her 2005 *Penelopiad*, "I've always been haunted by the hanging maids."[6] Indeed.

On this rereading, more even than on others, Odysseus's revenge seemed both excessive and unnecessary, based on the idea that the women have been corrupted by sexual contact with the suitors rather than, as seems far more likely, making do and surviving as best they could. The suitors staged orgies of maleness over which the maids had no control. And yet Odysseus coldly hanged them.

I've sentimentalized the *Odyssey* because it has always seemed more female, more romantic, and more domestic than epics like Homer's *Iliad* or Vergil's *Aeneid*.[7] It's also a prototype of the novel, my favorite genre. But the narrative has blood on its mind from the beginning. Far more unequivocally than the *Oresteia*, written hundreds of years later, the *Odyssey* states the characters' unqualified admiration for Orestes, who kills his mother and her lover to avenge his father, Agamemnon. It even sets up a partial parallel between these two sons of Greek warriors: Just as Orestes was right to kill his mother and his mother's lover, Telemachus can justly kill the suitors and their maids. In fact, the *Odyssey* yearns toward the vengeance with which it ends: slaughter, at a banquet, no less, as in a TV show like *Game of Thrones*. Violent revenge, served with relish.

Still, it's pretty great and almost infinitely evocative when, in dialogue with Athena, Telemachus says, "It's a wise child that knows his own father."[8] The line evokes the moment, familiar to many and certainly familiar to me, when we look in the mirror and see our father's or mother's faces looking back at us, as we remember them from childhood. We do a double-take—because that's us now. Or, more disturbingly, we hear the echo of our parent's voice in something we say and recognize an attitude we thought we had rejected.

On this rereading, I am left most with those haunting words: "It's a wise child that knows its own father." It's a wise daughter who knows her own mother. A wise person who knows herself. How much is such knowledge possible?

Missing Pictures

Asked what would you rescue first in a fire, once you were sure your family and pets are safe, most people would say: the family photographs. In war story after war story and Holocaust narrative after narrative, survivors tell how they hid and cherished the image of loved ones as a source of strength. People safe, animals found, most people would rescue the photo albums.

My mother threw out the family photographs when she was eighty-eight and in full *compos mentis*, an act so shocking that it opens up a window to what it means, for better and for worse, to be my mother's daughter.

The tale of the photographs begins when my mother found a new late-life partner in Joe, a neighbor who moved in downstairs about a year after my father died. Or, to put it more accurately, he found her. Joe Donna admired my mother's looks, her strength, her dignity, and her cooking, which remains legendary. My mother blossomed into his approval and became a softer, gentler version of the mother I knew, showing her teeth when she smiled, something I had never seen before.

At Rose's and Joe's late age, it's unclear how to characterize their bond: companionship, devoted friendship, true love, passion? Someone with whom to discuss the condition of the floors and the closets? The price of tomatoes and state of the fig tree that week? All of these apply. My mother and Joe shopped and cooked together regularly. Frugal both by temperament and necessity, they enjoyed comparing prices. They traveled together to Italy, where they presumably shared a room, but they lived in separate apartments until Joe lost his rent-stabilized place and my mother relocated with him to an apartment in the building next door. Even then, they maintained separate bedrooms, and that seemed important to my Mom. Her room displayed a familiar photo of my parents' wedding—my mother slim and gorgeous in a bias-cut satin gown and lustrous dark curls, my father tall and dapper, with a thin moustache and a languid Rudolph Valentino air. Joe's bedroom featured an image, taken long ago in Italy, of a younger version of himself, without glasses, next to a short, slightly plump woman wearing a lace mantilla. Joe's wife had been ill and institutionalized in New Jersey for many years; she died five years before he met my mother.

They had separate bedrooms, yet my mother's devotion to Joe had a mad, reckless, Anna Karenina air. They shared the kind of love people in their eighties devise—deep and bonded and something we should welcome, with or without sex. True love in late old age, fulfilled.

My brother's resistance to the whole arrangement was operatic. To Sal, resenting Joe seemed natural—as natural as being my father's son, though I suspect my father would have liked knowing that his Rose had company after he died. Joe's imprecations against my brother were operatic, too. So that what might have been a happy ending led to my brother's wrath. And a little murder.

One Thanksgiving at my brother's house, several years before my mother's death, she approached my husband after dinner, when she thought he'd be alone. Significantly, she did not choose me, but my husband. *Did we have any pictures of her and my father, especially the engagement picture*, she asked. He knew the one she meant, having seen it for years: a head-and-shoulders shot with her in a suave 1940s menswear suit and my father smiling, with his gold tooth showing. We didn't.

My husband is a nice guy, easier than I am and less likely to get angry. I came in on the conversation as he was wondering why she asked, since we were in New York and our photos likely to be in North Carolina. She told him that my brother wanted the engagement shot. When we assured her that it would be easy to duplicate and that we could do that for her, she confessed. *She didn't have the picture. She didn't have any of the family pictures. She'd thrown them out. She'd thrown them all out when she moved.* When we asked why, she said, "To spite your brother."

Now, my mother was a woman capable of nurturing a grudge in Greek or, in her case, southern Italian fashion. She never forgave her father for sending his family back to Italy for more than decade while he stayed in New York, a tale that may have included another woman, though, if so, I've never heard that voiced explicitly. Until the day my grandfather died, at 105, my mother remained fearful that her older sister, Caroline, would ask her to house him for part of the year, even though Caroline and her family lived in the prestigious Midwood area of Brooklyn, in a lovely large house purchased, at least in part, with my grandfather's cash.

That house formed a source of grievance for my mother as well, since she always regretted not owning one of her own. I recall how, shortly after my marriage, she gave up the second bedroom, which had been mine, to a landlord who wanted to expand his own apartment, offering as her reason the desire not to house my grandfather.[9] My mother also had never forgiven Caroline for having urged her to cut her hair at age sixteen, when she first came to Brooklyn. Her older sister told my mother she would look more "American" with a shorter do. Then she made fun of her new look, telling my mother that it made her look like a "gafoon" and a "greaseball."

My mother could certainly hold a grudge. But would she really throw out the family photos, without telling any of us, in a fit of pique because my brother opposed her moving in with Joe? Perhaps. I can imagine the pressure the decision to move placed on her and can see and hear her doing it: "It's a new apartment, after fifty years. Why do I need this junk?" Or "there's no room on these shelves" (in distress because the new place differed from the old) "so maybe I should just throw out the pictures." Or, "Sal would want them. Let him look for them then," as she tossed the photos in the garbage. There would be a certain grand Medea-like air to that last gesture that rings true.

But it's almost equally likely that a mistake was made and that she threw away the pictures by accident—in the same trash cans or at least the same location, I note for the record, that my favorite stuffed animal, named Ellie, found her end decades earlier. At a more sinister level, it's possible that Joe threw the photos away, knowingly, innocently, or some combination of the two, and that my mother was covering for him.

Either way, there are some big losers in this story: my brother and his son, me and my daughters, both of whom felt distraught when we learned that the family photos were gone. My girls had sat for many a day at my mother's apartment looking at her handsomely bound wooden albums, their pages lettered white on black in my father's well-rounded hand. My daughter Lizz had even told her grandma that, if she ever didn't want the photos, Lizz would. Yet if my mother was to be believed, she had tossed the pictures.

And then (and I'll stop here), there is the far more dramatic story of the ring—another and even more symbolic item with heavy family karma that says a whole lot about what it means to be my mother's daughter.[10]

After my mother died, my brother wouldn't help sort out her things because Joe would be in the apartment, its being his, too. I went with my family and looked, as my brother asked, for the three things he wanted: a small cross that hung over her sewing machine, the large cross that hung opposite her bed, and her gold wedding band. I found the first two easily. But the wedding band, which she'd worn on a chain around her neck the last times I remembered seeing it, was nowhere to be found. Without missing a beat, my brother Sal blamed Joe: He'd taken the ring and was hiding it, either as a keepsake or to sell for the gold. I believed that the ring had been lost or stolen in the hospital, nursing home, or hospice where our mother died. We went round and round this conversation on multiple occasions. But the actual explanation turned out to be more surprising.

For about three years after my mother died, Joe continued to live in their apartment, and my family would visit, often on a Sunday. He would usually serve his own simple specialty, which was meatballs, followed by cold cuts and then a plate of pastries from his favorite Eighteenth Avenue bakery. At one of these meals, I asked Joe about my mother's ring. Did he know where it was? Did he by any chance have it?

"The ring-a?" he asked, giving a shrug that indicated both an older Italian-American's knowledge and indifference. "Yeah, she sold-a it."

A stunning statement that needs some explanation.

From time to time, to fund his retirement, Joe would take pieces of gold jewelry he'd bought decades ago to a pawn shop. Not all the pieces were sold. He gave me a gold "M" pin after the first meal we had together; he gave my mother a gold necklace so gorgeous that, while she wore it daily, I am fearful of losing it and lock it away. One day, my mother went with Joe to the pawn shop and—as a lark, as a dare, as some symbolic expression—she asked the pawnbroker what he would give her for the ring. When he said fifty dollars, she made the deal.

Was her action Anna Karenina bravado? Perhaps—since she wouldn't truly need or especially value fifty dollars. Was it a goad, perhaps from Joe, who may have asked the pawnbroker half-jokingly or half-wickedly on my mother's behalf? Perhaps—I can imagine that, since there were sides to Joe I only rarely saw, and he had a vexed relationship with his only daughter, from whom he was estranged. Either way, this was reminiscent of the photos. There was a presence and then the trace of a presence. Then there was nothing, just the memory of the trace, discarded.[11]

I am trying here to evoke a mother and a grandmother good and even great by most standards. She cooked and cleaned and sewed with love; she always took excellent care of everything and everyone; she was never missing in action if you were sick or needed her. She is remembered warmly as a cook—hence the real but also sentimental value of her recipes. My daughters loved and honored her so strongly that, when my first granddaughter was born, my daughter Lizz knew immediately that she would be named in some way for Rose: Rosemary Jean, always called Rosie. But my mother also had a cold, unsentimental streak at the core.

When I was growing up, she'd criticize me in public for my pudginess and need for (how I cringed at the words) "a two-way stretch." She tended to compare me unfavorably to neighbors and to cousins who cooked and sewed; I, quite deliberately, did not. I always felt—though I now know I was wrong—that she wished I had been more like my adopted cousin Margaret: a pretty blonde who danced, married early, and almost immediately had two daughters. My mother's unsentimental nature made the tossing of the family photos and the pawning of the ring entirely possible, though such actions would ordinarily seem unlikely, even for a desperado.

My mother is the parent I most resemble, physically at least. That becomes truer and truer as I age into the years when I recall my mother best. Is there a way that I resemble this part of her, too?

Wars and Peace

In Tolstoy's *War and Peace*, which for years was my favorite novel, I love especially three scenes that are embarrassing by contemporary standards. All three refer to eternal time, and that spoke to me. But the real attraction was how they show warm families and cold families and the difference that makes for children. In the first scene, Prince Andrei, a naturally proud and cold person who has grown up in the household of an even prouder and colder father, has been wounded. Slightly earlier, Andrei turned away from life and almost courted death after his much younger fiancée, Natasha, fell in love with a cad her own age, who betrayed her. In the scene in question, Tolstoy renders Andrei's thoughts as he lies on the battlefield: "'Can this be death?' thought Prince Andrei, looking with a quite new, envious glance at the grass, the wormwood, and the streamlet of smoke that curled up from the rotating black ball. 'I cannot, I do not wish to die. I love life—I love the grass, this earth, this air.'" He feels "ecstatic pity and love" for his previous worst enemy, the man who stole Natasha. He grasps for the first time "love of our brothers, for those that love us and for those who hate us . . . that is what remained for me had I lived" (908).[12]

The passage shows Andrei's epiphany, a moment when he feels both intimately in love with nature and a detachment from former grievances. It makes the reader think that Andrei might survive to follow his new insights—except that he does not. Pages later in the novel, he dies, nursed by his sister and by Natasha, who has encountered him by chance. In the passage I quote, Tolstoy's narrator unabashedly says what he wants to say—sophistication be damned— and then kills off Andrei, as planned.

The second moment, a kind of pendant to the first and also a moment of epiphany, comes when Pierre (Prince Andrei's bumbling but avuncular friend) becomes a prisoner of war. He is tutored in how to survive by a peasant named Platon Karataev, idealized by Tolstoy as "an unfathomable, rounded, eternal personification of the spirit of simplicity and truth" (1078), a kind of noble savage. On a forced march during the winter, Platon cannot keep up, and the French shoot him. Pierre himself narrowly escapes execution. After both experiences, and like Andrei, Pierre feels joy when he looks at the sky: "'Life is everything. Life is God. Everything changes and moves and the movement is God. And while there is life there is joy in consciousness of the divine. To love life is to love God. Harder and more blessed than all else is to love this life in one's sufferings'" (1181). Embarrassing to our tastes and strongly didactic, the passage decants vintage Tolstoy. A feeling of oneness and harmony (the oceanic, I've called it in some of my work, and a feeling akin to that in meditation) washes over Andrei and Pierre when they look up at the sky. In Pierre's case, he lives to act on his realizations.

My final favorite passage in *War and Peace* is a more extended piece singled out by Georg Lukács, a beloved critic of the novel I've used many times in my work. In his early book *The Theory of the Novel*, Lukács used the scene as an example of bad writing but changed his mind over time and pronounced it (in his later book *Realism and the Novel*) his absolute favorite. The first epilogue in *War and Peace* sings a hymn to marriage. It was written when Tolstoy himself was newly wed, before his union with his wife disintegrated into an epic battle of wills that ended when he ran away from home one winter's night and died of pneumonia at a railway station. (If you've seen the film *The Last Station* [2009], it's an accurate rendering of memoirs about Tolstoy's death.)

In the epilogue, Natasha is a happy mother and fulfilled wife, jealous and possessive of Pierre, now her husband, who remains dedicated to his family. When the entire household gathers with relatives, they tolerate without notice the errors of Natasha's mother, the Old Countess, because she is old; not to do so would be cruel. The Old Countess, in turn, assesses her daughter's happiness with a knowing eye because "she had realized that all Natasha's outbursts had been due to her need of children and a husband"—in short, that Natasha is the kind of woman who needs a man to live life completely, a sentiment that I don't like on the surface because it sounds so sexist but does seem true for certain women.

In his youth, Pierre was overly abstract and unhappy; now he has become an exemplary husband and father, expressing the exuberance of family life by buying presents. My husband likes to compare himself to Pierre in this regard, just as I sometimes think that what the Old Countess said about Natasha, though I dislike it, is true of me.

I've homing in, through *War and Peace*, on some things it means to be my mother's daughter, things I learned both through books and meditation in the course of mourning. I need to get there.

Comedies of Error

I met my husband, Stuart, at Shakespeare in the Park—Central Park in New York, where the play that year was *A Comedy of Errors*. He was behind me and a friend on line, and, at the time, you waited for about an hour until tickets were handed out consecutively, so we both knew he'd be sitting next to us at the performance.

I was much infatuated that summer with a boy at school, away for the vacation. But I was with a friend who was unattached and, bolder than her, I kept talking to Stu and picked him up, for her. After the play, he walked us out of the park and took us for ice cream sodas. Despite strong hints from me, when we got on the train for Brooklyn, he accompanied me home, not her. It was far south in Brooklyn: Bensonhurst, a neighborhood where he'd never been. "Do people carry knives there?" he joked on the subway. Then he called me repeatedly that summer, arranging various treats—art films in Manhattan, off-off-Broadway plays, *Carmen* in box seats at the Met (a real splurge)—that I'd receive graciously but with a certain hauteur.

That fall, my college beau's former girlfriend returned from Paris, where she'd spent a year abroad living with another man. She was, he'd told me more than once, a famous admiral's daughter and (as he'd not told me) blond, perky, and petite, the physical antithesis of me. Romance with me was off the table, finally and absolutely. He thought Stu would be good for me, someone who would not reinforce my (and his) natural tendency to think too much—a presumptuous assumption if there ever was one. Years later, when I met this man again by chance and we had lunch, he was living with a woman named Muffy who was, he repeated several times with emphasis, the daughter of the Episcopal bishop for a nearby large city. I recalled his earlier girlfriend and the way he'd talked about her and especially her admiral of a father—and the pieces began to fit.

A famous admiral I later saw testifying on TV; the Episcopal bishop of a city where such things really matter: I suddenly understood why it would never have worked between me and him. We had talked long hours about books and ideas and marveled at how much we had in common and how we loved to be together. He called me his soul mate. But I was a working-class scholarship girl, the daughter of a dressmaker and an office worker. He was a Catholic born in Levittown, a suburb less grand than I thought at the time. I realize now, though I did not realize it then, that while I was moving up through education ("crossing Ocean Parkway," I call it in an earlier memoir), he was doing his own version by trying, through marriage, to make it into the high-caste WASP establishment.

I don't know if he married Muffy and they bought a townhouse near Rittenhouse Square and lived happily ever after. I've sometimes thought that he may have died young, since I've never seen or heard from him after a few chance encounters and would have expected somehow to meet. He had scars on his wrists when I knew him—a motorcycle accident, he said, though a suicide attempt seemed far more likely. He had bad acid trips and fires in his apartment and other unexplained events in the years I knew him. I hope life did not end for him in one of those ways. I wish him well and always did. But I now see that he would never have been the right man for me. A marriage to him would not have lasted. With him, I never would have become myself. We were perhaps too similar to be lifelong best friends and mates.

That fall, I took up with Stu. What might have been a rebound romance morphed into a very long-term marriage. At first, I thought it was a weird union of convenience. Being Italian, my parents wouldn't let me leave the house until I was married. After we'd dated for a while, they invited Stu's parents over, on their own, and more or less arranged our wedding. Stu and I were both bemused. It was a time when writing your own vows was the rage, so we let it be, promising each other "affection, friendship, and understanding"—but nothing more. I remember how we wanted to marry at the Ethical Culture building on Prospect Park West, but our parents vetoed that, selecting instead an Italian restaurant midway between Stu's neighborhood and mine that, ironically, was later the scene of my mother's funeral lunch. The pastor from Ethical Culture presided, filling in our bare-bones vows with the story of Ruth, which seemed right, since we'd provided a meager ceremony for our guests.

For several years, we would renew a contract, always aware that either of us could walk away from the marriage with no hard feelings. After a while, we dropped the habit. And here we are, decades later, with two daughters and a mostly harmonious relationship, not without its warts, for sure, but one in which we share a lot of values, common interests, and sustained passion. And yet, if asked—as I was just the other month—why I married my husband, I say I don't know and invoke my parents.

Why not just say, *love*? Why not just say, *fun and chemistry*? Why maintain the aura of a diva long after the role fits? If I can extend a bouquet to my husband, via writing, I do that here.

Thinking back, I'd say I've been my mother's daughter. The way her emotions played out influence the way I show affection too. I'd say as well that awareness of how my birth family controlled its feelings forms the real reason that I married Stu. He's from a less orderly family but also a more openly loving one: the kind of family where everyone is thought the smartest, the most talented, the most beautiful. It's a pattern that runs all the way through his aunts, his uncles, his sister—all openly adoring. I wanted that kind of unconditional approval. I wanted that kind of warmth in my marriage. I have conveyed that kind of feeling, I honestly believe, to my children. It's got good karma and just plain feels good. I'd never throw away the family photos or the wedding rings. Never. And we have, collectively, made sure that we all have copies of the pictures, just in case of that hypothetical fire.

5
College Teaching and Culture Wars or: What Really Happened at Duke

A few years after getting tenure at Duke University, when I was in my mid-thirties, I became the associate chair of my department for seven very full years. During this time, people chatted in the halls, and conversations overflowed about ideas, books, classes, and, yes, local gossip. We mounted monthly colloquia presenting faculty work in progress so that, as does not always happen, we knew our colleagues' current passion projects. Lecture halls were packed with visitors, some of them future colleagues, like Henry Louis (Skip) Gates Jr. and Eve Kosofsky Sedgwick. I joined a prolific writing group with other women in which we produced some of our favorite work.[1] For me, it was academic nirvana.

Along with top-ranked faculty, from 1991 to 1995, Duke English had an excellent and equally powerful set of graduate applications, with some 71 percent of new PhDs hired into tenure-track positions; that number dropped the following year, but only to 60 percent.[2] Undergraduate students felt proud to study English, with record numbers of majors. As associate chair, I oversaw all new hiring and internal decisions for the department, so that, after seven years, I had either hired or promoted at least half the department. I assumed— correctly for a good long while—that I'd banked a lot of good will.

Just four years later and shortly after I became chair, I found my picture on the front page of the *New York Times*, and not at all in the way that one imagines. Under the headline "Discord Turns Academe's Hot Team Cold," a male colleague accused me of "mismanagement," which made the whole thing sound racy or even criminal, though it was not even remotely like that. What happened? And what has happened since?

During the heady period when English and critical theory were power disciplines, my friend and chairman was Stanley Fish, a provocateur by nature and a lightning rod for publicity, which the department received in abundance. When he bought a vacation house in rural New York, a friendly colleague quipped, "Who's going to interview him way up there? The cows?" Soon we attracted the attention of conservative think tanks that funded workshops for academics who opposed change, especially regarding what were called critical theory and canon revision; the inclusion of more texts by women and minorities and in popular genres; and the encouragement of stylistic changes such as personal and experimental writing. Duke English participated fully in the 1990s culture wars, and it became a favorite target.

With some regularity, the English Department got accused of undermining tradition and thereby corrupting not just higher education but also the nation's moral values. At one point, the university asked me to appear on national TV and urged me to say, as often as possible, that students do study Shakespeare at Duke. The interview lasted three hours, and I was quoted for perhaps four minutes (all that I expected), saying—you guessed it—that students do study Shakespeare at Duke.

Perhaps inevitably, the department's reputation polarized its members. Some people loved critical theory, memoir, postcolonialism, African American studies, queer studies that challenged heterosexuality as a norm, and work that was public-facing and for general audiences. Others felt concerned that literary history and close reading, the forms of scholarship we had learned in graduate school, were being undervalued. Some people changed sides. Frank Lentricchia, for example, an Americanist who helped bring Stanley Fish and Fredric Jameson to campus, prominently moved from riding the theory train to derailing it. Initially a friend (and *paisano!*), he switched, it seemed to me on a dime, to being a fierce enemy. Our last genial lunch was at a local restaurant where I gave him a gift for his newborn daughter. After that, I started receiving angry, sometimes even threatening e-mails. Could they really be about internal politics, I wondered, some of which he'd raised at lunch? Was I a proxy target for Stanley Fish? Or, as I thought in my lighter moments, had he not liked the gift?

Even as people at Duke published their work on bestsellers, film, TV, and popular genres like sci-fi, music videos, and (later) gaming, other scholars objected and stood in defense of standard historical periods and established texts. A frequently invoked but increasingly shaky standard for what was worthy of study was what the nineteenth-century essayist Matthew Arnold called "the test of time," usually defined as fifty years. At a more pork-chop level, some colleagues resented the higher salaries and other perquisites awarded to national and international stars. Since some, even many, of those stars were Black or queer (none were both), over time resentments festered and spilled over onto those categories, sometimes consciously and sometimes not.

Right before I became chair, the department disagreed strongly about a hire; the debate was badly bungled by a scholar of eighteenth-century literature (now deceased) who briefly led the department after Stanley Fish decided not to continue in that role. During the three years of this man's leadership, many in the department moved into ventures of their own, becoming, in effect, free agents and independent contractors.[3] Divisions that Stanley Fish had papered over deepened into chasms. After department meetings, I'd sometimes meet Stanley on our way to the parking lot, and he'd say, "It's like watching the grass grow, isn't it?" or "That grass is getting high now." I agreed but sometimes suggested using the mower.

When a tenure-track position opened in Renaissance studies, a man who proudly claims descent from Genghis Khan and his then wife (who wrote on Lady Macbeth) thought that she would be hired instead of the out lesbian who was also applying for the position. Given the vacillations of our then chair, the couple may have received a promise that was not the chair's to give. Against some advice, I decided to back the lesbian candidate at our hiring meeting because her work seemed to me more promising. That decision formed a turning point in my life.

The debacle-in-waiting crystallized when, upon becoming chair before an external departmental review, I tried — foolishly, it seems now — to appoint two of my more conservative colleagues to be my associate chair and director of graduate studies: "reaching across the aisle," as it were, a gesture both refused. I also tried to retain three prominent colleagues in queer studies, Eve Sedgwick, Michael Moon, and Jonathan Goldberg, by moving Moon and Goldberg from the English department into Literature, then a program sometimes used to ease tensions.[4] Several male colleagues wrote extremely nasty letters to the administration that made Goldberg and Moon decide they would not change departments after all but instead change universities. The same male colleagues led a concerted effort to badmouth me during the review, which ultimately tried to thread the needle, reporting that some people opposed and no longer trusted me but finding no actual misdeeds.

After the review became public, the same men piled on me in the student newspaper. I had just seen a copy, when Stanley Fish called to commiserate. I was crying and could not hide my tears. The next day, he tried to defend me in the paper and received similar abuse, deciding soon afterward to leave Duke. I was in London when he called to tell me that he was sorry to add to my troubles, but he was definitely going. I of course understood. But his departure made what had been a painful but local kerfuffle—my colleagues at Duke knew, of course, and my children had heard about it at school—into national news, covered not just on the front page of the *New York Times* but in *Lingua Franca*, a journal about academia then widely read. I was grateful when the *Chronicle of Higher Education* pretty much ignored the issue.

I cannot fairly assess the extent to which my being a woman, and ethnic, contributed to the way I was perceived and treated. I was considered aggressive, unfair, manipulative, and unworthy of defense in public, a litany familiar to recent female politicians and conforming to gender stereotypes as they appear in language. I was also the first woman in my department to have a baby, the first woman to chair my department in modern memory, and widely perceived as Jewish, even though I was raised and remain to some extent Catholic. In academia, we all know of chairs and even university presidents who fail badly but whose positions are routinely renewed and spared public embarrassment; I was not even given the chance to resign. Though I was widely perceived to have been replaced, I functioned as chair until the end of my term, which could not have come quickly enough as far as I was concerned.[5]

Like my family, I have a stoic side to my personality, and it showed on this occasion. I thought a lot about the many conversations my parents had had at our dinner table about the dangers of my father's accepting promotions at work that might cost him friends. I had accepted a promotion. It had cost me friends. Out of pride, out of a perverse sense of omertà, or out of a pragmatic desire not to make daily life any worse than it already was, I never revealed that my dean and provost had in fact encouraged every step I took to retain distinguished colleagues—even meeting furtively with me on weekends to make and encourage my plans—and then left me holding the bag.

When I was interviewed by the *New York Times*, I chose not to badmouth my department by calling out its forms of homophobia, intellectual conservatism, and the poor behavior of some of my colleagues—not to mention their suspiciousness or outright hostility toward an ethnic female. In a different essay, I would add racism to that already bulky list, since some of the same colleagues who attacked me petitioned the administration first not to hire and then not to retain two of the nation's most noted Black scholars.[6] Once again, this is *a lot*, all of it at odds with Duke University's reputation as a first-rate national and not just a first-rate Southern university. An institution, I should add, that has treated me well on many occasions—though obviously not this one—and that I love.

After this bona fide, real-life *disgrazia*, I reacted almost exactly as my parents would have done: in public, with a proud refusal to seem needy or the object of pity, and, in private, with mortification that went all the way to shame. For reasons of sheer self-interest, I should have stayed out of the original hiring dispute far more than I did, or at least kept my mouth shut, since I have, after all, read *Macbeth*. When my queer studies colleagues wanted to leave, I probably should have let them, though I still think I did the right thing in trying to retain valued friends and scholars. As the wonderful, now deceased Eve Sedgwick put it at the time in a phone call, "There are some train wrecks worth having." There are. There really are. Though it's much better not to be tied to the tracks.

The year of and after the debacle, I worked hard for the department, negotiating an unprecedented eight job offers, of which three were accepted by prominent people: Houston Baker, Maureen Quilligan, and Priscilla Wald. That was a deliberate decision, one I considered a form of public redemption (quite Catholic of me, really), for having failed to better manage my term as chair. It still took a few years to be heard when I spoke at meetings, for everyone to greet me when we passed on the Quad, and generally to feel respected and seen. One of my few positive memories of this year was the visible joy on the face of an African American assistant dean when he congratulated me on the main dean's announcement in the student newspaper of all eight offers. It was sweet and appreciated, though I knew it was too soon, for the main dean went on to offer some of the candidates lowball salaries, what I jokingly called "offers they could not accept."

If I could advise my earlier self, striding through Duke's halls with blithe confidence, I would caution her about trying to shape a department in ways that suited her own affinities in thought and style. One person with whom I am now quite friendly called me a "partisan" at the time—and I was. I liked my department's high national ranking, our sense of energy, our meetings and debates and colloquia; I wanted to sustain and grow them all. Many wanted a quieter, less avant-garde place. Knowing what I know now, I might tell myself not to become the chair at all or, at least, to do less to irritate people. During this period, I cried at home daily but behaved in public as bravely as I could. The knots I felt in my innards may yet shorten my life.

I could say more and name more names, but I don't need or even want to do that. The information is readily available to anyone who wants it, and I still work with some of these people, with whom I sometimes agree. When I travel and meet other colleagues, the vagaries of memory often run like this: "I remember that you were involved in something at Duke. I can't quite recall. You saved your department, right?" To which I smile like Mona Lisa.

Affinities

I could illustrate how culture wars past and present play out in universities in different ways. Quite notably, for example, African American and Black studies critique aspects of America's past and present and include experimental writing and public-facing work, like TV appearances or documentaries, that can generate pushback. So does some work in gender and sexuality, feminism, and on the environment. People follow different tracks to innovate within academia, which may or may not cohere into a movement or field. The most pertinent path connected to "what really happened at Duke" was the then new field called queer studies, with its frequent impulses toward experimental style and memoir and its challenge to heterosexuality as a norm. At Duke, and still today, the field is associated with the superstar Eve Kosofsky Sedgwick, who was at the center of the storm at Duke this chapter has narrated and who died in 2009 of breast cancer. So, then, a little about Eve.

While we were never intimate friends, I always found Eve a warm and genial colleague, someone who would open her house to anyone and often did. I remember one fun tradition she inaugurated, at which we donated clothing and accessories to graduate students right before our annual professional meeting, the Modern Language Association, at a social evening cum thrift shop. For me, Eve was always an excellent colleague, someone responsive to students and reliable on committees. Someone with a very strong but not unfair mind. She suffered no fools and that showed at times, so that some people felt differently. At one of her lectures, for example, an older colleague asked how straight white males like him should receive her work; Eve smiled, said thank you—then turned her head and asked for the next question. The older colleague asked a foolish question; Eve showed disdain. The exchange forms a miniature of what was happening in the department; this kind of struggle was also visible in the elections of 2016 and 2020, as different groups fought not just for power but also for respect.

Eve Sedgwick was very public about having breast cancer and about undergoing treatment for the recurrence that would, in time, kill her. I was the chair of a fractious department. When I asked one colleague, in private, to tone down the scorn he heaped on Eve at department meetings, he asked why. I replied that she had cancer, was undergoing chemotherapy, and could use less stress. He looked at me and said, "No, of course not. Someone is always dying of cancer." To which there can truly be no response. You get the idea. I got the idea. Eve got the idea. Citing the desire to be near her husband, who lives in New York, Eve left the next year for the City University of New York's Graduate Center, where she was a brilliant and colorful, even eccentric presence—though never less than electric—who wove textiles and taught that skill.

Eve's first book was *The Coherence of Gothic Conventions*, followed by *Between Men* and *The Epistemology of the Closet*. While foundational to gender and queer studies, *Between Men* and *The Epistemology of the Closet* consist mostly of scholarly close readings, albeit written with flair. Later work was more deliberately provocative, like *Tendencies* and *A Dialogue on Love*.[7] I don't think it would be wrong to see a good-girl, bad-girl dynamic I recognize in my own life operating in her career. At first, a reasonably cautious meeting of academic norms, followed by a certain, eagerly embraced edginess. While many academics break loose after tenure or promotion to full professor, some queer scholars do so dramatically.

I discern similar patterns in the careers of other colleagues I know in queer studies, for example, Wayne Koestenbaum, and others I do not know, like Marjorie Garber, Terry Castle, Hilton Als, Jack Halberstam, and Karen Tongson.[8] My teaching life having been kind, it also appears in recent publications by former students like Jacob Tobia, the author of *Sissy: A Coming of Gender Story* and a prominent speaker on gender-queer identity, and Andrea Chu, the author of *Females: A Concern* and a trans woman who has been profiled in *New York Magazine* and is writing a commissioned book of essays for a major press.[9] More traditional work, followed by more personal, experimental work was the usual pattern; now, following the trail blazed by their elders, the current, younger generation sometimes skips the more traditional step or opts out of academia entirely.

Sedgwick's essays were often especially bold and provocatively titled, like "Jane Austen and the Masturbating Girl," which got a lot of attention at the Modern Language Association. Some were fully scholarly in approach, situating themselves within philosophical and psychological debates; I think of "Paranoid Reading and Reparative Reading, or, You're So Paranoid, You Probably Think This Essay Is about You."[10] Others were provocative in more than title, like "How to Bring Your Kids Up Gay," a title that raised eyebrows in 1991.[11] Others are full-tilt autobiographical and sometimes even a revelation: "A Poem Is Being Written" and her explorations of women, chemotherapy, fantasies of physical degradation, and the abject in work like *A Dialogue on Love*.[12]

Would the academy have moved so quickly to accept and welcome queer theory without someone like Eve Sedgwick? Would recent graduates like Jacob Tobia and Andrea Chu have mapped their gender-queer and trans identities and written their work so soon after college? Perhaps. But I believe it would have taken longer. The arrival of queer studies and models like Sedgwick, Koestenbaum, and others helped foster changes within academia that also accelerated changes in national values. Certainly, it coincides with the period when homosexuality moved from being quasi-secret for many in mainstream America, to having legal recognition and protection. Queer scholars' pivot toward personal, sensuous, revealing, juicy, *embodied* criticism and writing mirrors my own pivot into genres and styles also favored by Italian-American academic women, who were also fairly new to the academy during those years.

Italianità

My full name, Marianna De Marco Torgovnick, contains a host of histories, including the vagaries of immigration and the interplay of Italian- and Jewish-Americans. It does not appear on any of my degrees or on any of my books, except for the first edition of *Crossing Ocean Parkway* and, now, *Crossing Back*. In between, I asked the publisher of *Crossing Ocean Parkway* to remove my middle name from subsequent editions, as well as to delete the subtitle, *Readings by an Italian American Daughter*. Why?

The first half of the book was written from a point of view that hovers between my teenage self, who believed that my parents were hostile to my going to college, and my adult self, who realizes that could not, in fact, have been the case. As I say in *Crossing Ocean Parkway*, my mother feared that college would lead me out of Bensonhurst and away from her world, which in fact proved the case; my father remained proud of what he perceived to be my aberrant success at school. But in my family, a covert matriarchy, I would never have been allowed to go to college if my mother had been unwilling.

I received a lot of fan mail about that book, especially from women and from Southern males who identified with my divided loyalties. But I also received a surprising amount of hate mail, all of it from Italian-American men who believed I was disparaging Italian-Americans. My now-retired paisano colleague often said things like "nice haircut. It makes you look less Jewish"; he may also have felt that I disparaged Italian-Americans.

One of the funniest, but also painful, exchanges was with a librarian (if I recall correctly) who represented a fraternal group of Italian-American professionals in upstate New York. He read *Crossing Ocean Parkway* as "a mystery story" (his words), asking: Why do I say that Italian-Americans discourage higher education for their daughters? Why did I feel the need to imp onto Jewish culture? Why am I ashamed of being Italian? Why do I resent being Italian-American? The last questions threw me, since I don't feel at all ashamed or resent being Italian-American. Over a period of months, I replied to several letters from this man, who was hectoring me like a drunk at a comedy club, until he asked two more questions: Why do I say that relatively few Italian-American women have written books? (It was, remember, 1994, when relatively few Italian-American women *had* published novels or nonfiction, let alone literary criticism.)[13] Then, the culminating taunt, what about the many fine Italian-American women who have written *cookbooks*?

I stopped answering at that point, and the letters stopped coming. But a peculiar pattern that other female colleagues noticed as well persisted on Amazon: Every time a high rating appeared for *Crossing Ocean Parkway*, a really low one would offset it, with these almost always outraged, just outraged, that a professor of English at Duke University would write such a book—the kind of identification that the average Amazon reviewer would not make. I was being trolled by conservative think tanks in the culture wars; such comments were often posted by Italian-American men.

By 2021, there are many more female Italian-American college teachers, with the women less commonly disguised—as I am—by their married names. In general, Italian-Americans have gone mainstream, with female stars like Madonna and Lady Gaga and powerful politicians like Nancy Pelosi. During 2020, I admired how Anthony Fauci handled the COVID-19 crisis, consolidating the sense that Italian-Americans now anchor American life.

But even *way back then*, in 1994, there were still some Italian-American women who, whether younger or older, wrote fiction, creative nonfiction, or memoir, genres where I work too: among the older, Helen Barolini, Sandra (Mortola) Gilbert, and Louise DeSalvo come to mind, as does the agent provocateur Camille Paglia, about whom I have written negatively in the past.[14] Just my age and my fellow member in my long-lived writing group, there is Cathy (Notari) Davidson, whose writing and Futures Initiative at the City University of New York's Graduate Center push consistently to reimagine the university and to experiment with and change pedagogical styles. Several others are younger: for example, the journalist and author Maria Laurino and the memoirist and writer of creative nonfiction Mary Cappello. Though my writing took me in different directions after *Crossing Ocean Parkway*, and though I have never thought of other Italian-American women as influences, these women share my attraction to memoir and personal writing, and they have published far more than my upstate correspondent's "cookbooks."

The closest connection, almost an older sister separated at birth, is Louise DeSalvo, who taught at Hunter and lived in New Jersey until her death in 2018. In fact, DeSalvo was a kind of intellectual alter ego, writing, "the unlikely narrative of how a working-class Italian girl became a critic and a writer,"[15] a narrative more recently told in fiction by Elena Ferrante in *My Brilliant Friend*. In other books, DeSalvo writes about moving houses, writing as self-healing, and food—all preoccupations to which I gravitated in *Crossing Back*. The ambiance of DeSalvo's childhood home was quite different from mine—more volatile, more febrile, more marked by depression—so that there are major differences in both our memories and in our approach. Still, despite the differences, like other Italian-American female writers, DeSalvo and I clearly handle similar themes and share a style that includes personal voice and embodied criticism.[16]

Mary Cappello states the goal of composing "essays, memoir, literary non-fiction and experiments in prose, always with the aim of bringing a poetic sensibility into concert with scholarly ethos."[17] In an interview, Cappello says that she remains "suspicious of the easy bow to protocol,"[18] a fine thing for a writer and more rather than less typical of Italian-American academic women, who often had to be assertive, not shy, about their intellectual interests. Cappello's *Night Bloom* is an unconventional memoir structured not just around her own memories of growing up as a lesbian but around flowers, her grandfather's journal, and her mother's poems. *Life Breaks: A Mood Almanack* announces itself as a book that does not "start at point A, take you by the hand, and carefully lead you to point B," proudly proclaiming its unconventional self.[19]

In fact, many Italian-American women who teach college and write—including DeSalvo, Cappello, Laurino, and me—share impulses so similar as to suggest, deep down, at least one strong link: a push-pull relationship to Italian-American female identity, at least some of which must be rejected for the writer to become herself. As I say in *Crossing Ocean Parkway*, "If adolescents need rebellion, female adolescents in Bensonhurst need it even more" (162).

Maria Laurino nails it in *Old World Daughter, New World Mother*:

> I am a descendant of people who believed in the primacy of family, who understood that the greatest moral, spiritual, and emotional satisfaction is derived from caring for others, especially the young and the old. They also believed in the evil eye and kept women out of the basement for fear that their menstrual blood would spoil the fermenting wine.[20]

The first sentence lures us in with the enveloping warmth of the Italian family, *la famiglia*. The second sentence zaps us where we live, or lived, in a culture that often deemed us inferior or troublesome because we did not have a penis. A similar push-pull relationship to Italian-American culture shows up in DeSalvo's work, with her mother and father's chronic rage and disarray, and in Cappello's references to family dysfunction, "the patriarchal heritage of Mediterranean culture," and the "impending violence" she experienced in her youth.[21]

Growing up Italian-American and female often meant growing up scrappy, self-assertive, and devoted to education as a way of moving up and out. While not unknown for men and women from privileged, mainstream backgrounds, a similar struggle for identity is more common among working-class ethnics, racial minorities, and LGBTQ people. What does that pattern predict about a career as a college teacher and writer? As in queer studies, for the first generation of Italian-American women who teach college, it has meant writing to "heal" (as in DeSalvo's *Vertigo* and *Writing as a Way of Healing*), to identify the self (as in Laurino), to "claim the awkward over [easy] revelation" (as in Cappello), to change the academy (as in Gilbert and Davidson), sometimes to raise a middle finger (as in Paglia). Many combine good-girl and bad-girl instincts: good enough not to get fired and to get tenure, bad enough to sometimes be at odds with their departments, institutions, or profession.

Are all academic Italian-American women alike? No, of course not. I studied, for example, with Joan Ferrante at Columbia University, and she remained a mainstream Dante scholar. Even in the group mentioned here, I bristle at some of Maria Laurino's writing, for example about Bensonhurst—home of Tony Manero in the film *Saturday Night Fever* (1977) and the scene of the racially motivated murder of Yusuf Hawkins in 1989. Laurino identifies Bensonhurst with Italian-American stereotypes but feels able to escape, while, having been born and lived there until I married at age nineteen, I cannot.[22] Nonetheless, since Laurino *thinks* about Italian-American identity in terms of Bensonhurst stereotypes that intellectuals must avoid, she shares at least some of my and DeSalvo's and Cappello's ambivalent feelings about how working-class Italian-American culture plays out for ambitious women. Or, since we are in 2021, let's use a hopeful past tense: *played out*.

College Teaching Today

In 2020, right after the pandemic hit, Duke University froze salaries, benefits, and hiring, as a way to avoid layoffs or furloughs. So did many other colleges and universities. Shortly thereafter, the university announced new "cluster hires": two people in Latinx studies and two in Asian-American studies, taking some care to explain that the funding came from special sources. On a Zoom call with full professors, the dean announced that next year, there would be a similar search in Indigenous studies. Duke's "two plus two" format suggests some weird Noah's Ark analogy, but, to my surprise, no one at the meeting or, later, in my department objected to the special emphasis on representing fields and groups underpopulated on Duke's faculty, fields that reflect demographics from which Duke increasingly draws its students. As a sidebar here,

Duke has long supported, in multiple ways, African American and African studies, in part because Duke recognizes its past as a Southern university that ended segregation rather late in the day, as well as the conspicuous portion of its janitorial and food service staff that is Black.

When asked, I was pleased to serve on my departmental search committee for the hires in Latinx, where I learned a lot about a previously unfamiliar field—including that the term itself is disputed.[23] Much of what I learned related to embodied criticism today. Of interest, given my own background, a number of candidates attended a community college before, say, Berkeley, Yale, or Cornell for their BA and graduate degrees, with some announcing themselves as first-generation college and even first-generation high school. Neither of my parents finished middle school, so I could identify with that. But the most striking aspect of Latinx studies today connects directly to the stylistic experimentation, personal voice, and embodied criticism that increasingly made its way into the academy in the 1990s. In addition to traditional literary or cultural criticism, a surprising percentage of young Latinx scholars write poetry, memoir, and creative nonfiction—two out of three not uncommon, and sometimes all three. In short, the development of this new academic cohort parallels, to a striking extent, what we have seen in other groups new to academia, with the partial difference that these applicants are often younger scholars, most of them untenured.

While all had published or were working on a research monograph, they were upfront, early in their careers, about their other interests, as older generations sometimes were not. Older generations of embodied, public-facing critics have influenced the kind of work that does and does not count toward hiring, tenure, and promotion at colleges and universities. In turn, this new generation will expand networks of mentoring, influence, and what college teachers can do. They also will interact with, and often rebut, current versions of the culture wars, which tend to cluster around issues of immigration: who counts as "a real American" and deserves respect. Work on subjects like migration can be surprising and unexpected: the influence of card games like *loteria* in the arts, for example, and culturally different ways to analyze risk.[24]

The end of my own story has taken a few similarly unanticipated turns. In 1999, I needed, as they say, to get out of Dodge. When I was asked to replace a colleague teaching Duke in New York who couldn't do it at the very last minute, I accepted, though I ordinarily would not have done so. Two years later, a brave Midwestern university made me an offer that seemed too good to turn down until Duke (in the person of the same dean who had trashed me) proposed that, if I stayed, I could more or less permanently direct a program in New York each fall. Because I got to *choose* whether to remain at Duke, it became easier to let go of the past. Painful as they were, without the incidents narrated here, I would never have gotten to teach and then to direct Duke in New York, an arts and media program that has become an important part of my professional life.

As a teacher in and director of this program, I have sent many wonderful students into the world in TV, film, theater, writing, law, medicine, business, and more. I'm proud of these students and of the deep immersion in the arts they've brought with them into later life, something they tell me has enriched it. Doing the program yearly also gave my life a New York dimension that I had always wanted but never thought possible. Among the many losses of the 2020–2021 pandemic has been New York's rich cultural life, which now seems like a fairy tale. New York being New York, I have faith that it will come back.

In turn, being away from campus each fall and then summer allowed me to develop a detached, Zen-like attitude toward departmental politics that is the professional version of what I call memory without pain. At department meetings, I cite facts, give my opinions, sometimes even (being me) make proposals, but I accept all the group's votes with equanimity—"witnessing" the results, rather than feeling emotionally involved. While I have enjoyed payback when it's come my way without especially malign actions (I am, after all, half Sicilian), I truly feel no hatred toward anyone involved in "what really happened at Duke."

I continue to teach in the English department, which has changed over time, with misogyny now pretty much unknown, homophobia and racism far less visible, and intellectual conservatism at least up for discussion. English and theory are no longer power disciplines, and the halls are much quieter, with faculty mostly working from home, even before the pandemic. The number of majors and graduate students is much reduced, as is typical nationwide. But, and this has been wonderful, I have many new colleagues who know that *something* dramatic and messy happened in the department's past but never seem to associate it with me—unless I tell them.

6

Elephants: A Meditation on Mortality

Though my parents were working class and very careful about money, they stocked my early years with a variety of stuffed animals and dolls. Everywhere I looked—on the bed, on the bureau, on shelves, on the floor—stuffed animals and doll-babies stood guard. Bunnies from Easter, including Harry Belabunny, a riff on Harry Belafonte. A variety of teddy bears. A whole passel of cute females. Ensconced in the place of honor at the head of the bed, the reigning favorite was a bride doll in a long white gown, for which my mother had sewn a matching turquoise bridesmaid's dress that presaged at least three bridesmaid's dresses in my future. The doll had short dark hair and Sarah Palin wink-wink eyes. If she had a name, I don't recall. I was supposed to love her. But a secret lay buried in my heart.

I didn't like the bride doll all that much. She seemed to me too fussy, too perfect, too angular, and too designed to predict a woman's fate that I already, at age five, must have been resisting, just a little. My mother didn't know my feelings about the doll, and I would not have told her—for anything, for almost. My secret love was Ellie, the stuffed elephant I'd had for as long as I could remember. Perhaps ten inches tall and wide of girth, her classic gray plush had worn thin over the years, no doubt by hugging. Her floppy ears were lined in red (not pink, but fading toward that shade). Her tail long gone, two white strings dangled out to mark the spot. My Ellie.

One day, when I was about five or six, we had new neighbors, and the mother, who had a daughter a little younger than me, came over for the classic Italian-American coffee and cake. When she saw my room, the little girl went green and my mother—a good mom but not notable then or ever for sensitivity or sentimentality—suggested that I give her one of my stuffed animals or dolls. I froze, doubtful about the plan. Intending to inflict no harm, my mother suggested that we give the neighbor child Ellie.

Always wanting to seem well behaved and generous, I clenched myself tight and said nothing. But as soon as the neighbors left and the door closed, I immediately collapsed into tears and confessed how much I valued Ellie, how much I'd miss Ellie, how much I *loved* Ellie. I told my mother, sincerely, that I could lose anything else and not care—even the bride doll: a fact that made her blink. Pragmatic and strong, my mother swung into immediate action, offering me a few options and taking the one I chose—a ragged baby doll of some sort (she peed!)—immediately went down to the neighbor's apartment. She went to make a trade but returned with shocking news.

Our neighbors owned a German shepherd who, in the space of perhaps fifteen minutes, had already had his way with Ellie. She'd been torn to shreds and was no longer in a position to be given back to anyone. When I visited her later that day in the trash, her gray velvet was sloppily hewn through, but her ears were intact and her sad two-thread tail still said "Hi, there." I wanted to retrieve her, but my mother convinced me I should not; she was garbage now and so clearly just a remnant of her former self. We put her in a box and left her there, with gravity—a funeral of sorts, and the first one I attended— though I wish I'd saved her.

I always remembered Ellie and found it odd that, in apartment after apartment and finally in the house where I raised my daughters, I always had bathrooms in colors that I professed to dislike but never changed: pink and gray or black. My Ellie.

When I told my husband and daughters about Ellie, I began to receive many a wooden elephant and marble elephant, many a metal or glass elephant, many an elephant mobile, bracelet, pendant, box, tray, coasters, or toss pillows, two in a hip Brooklyn fabric that still adorn my bedroom. Surrounded now by elephants given to me by those I love, I feel bolstered and protected— though none, of course, has even come close to replacing Ellie.

I've added to the ensemble, which has turned into something of a fetish. Small framed postcards of Babar that I used in the bathrooms of my first New York apartments. (And yes, I know that there's a bathroom theme here.) Had the tiles been pink and gray and black, like the bathrooms in the first two apartments I rented, would I have needed them? A slider bracelet of elephants I bought at Opryland in Nashville, augmented by others I buy on eBay and wear every day to offset the original bracelet's loss. Golden or painted Ganeshas I buy in shops and on New York City streets, elevated into a collection. Raising the question: Can one make up for loss by buying? No, when the loss is a family member. Can't be done. All that ever remains is a stash of memories. Yes and no, when the loss is an old stuffed elephant.

When I mention my elephant fetish to people I know, they often surprise me by matching my elephant love to even more elephant love. A famous writer with a similar collection, a businessman who spends vacations at an elephant hospital in Thailand, a colleague from Africa who bonds over my elephant slider bracelet and tells me that her husband's chosen totem animal is the elephant. Practically everyone in India adores Ganesh the elephant god, making offerings when they open businesses, move, marry, travel, and, above all, begin books. All kinds of people high and low buy elephant jewelry, pillows, and statues—an extravagant outpouring of affection that finds its way into merchandise, a factor that is not ultimately insignificant. In fact, have you ever heard someone say that they hate elephants? It's rare, if ever.

For the most part, we think of elephants as peaceable creatures with contented habits. Our affections favor the idea of loving and loveable elephants, bypassing all the messiness visible around the actual beasts—no dirty straw, no smells and breakage. Despite occasional instances of elephant rage, in Shana Alexander's words, "No animal has been more beloved than the elephant by all the peoples and cultures who have known him, and I know of no legends, myths, or folklore of evil." In fact and fiction, "the animal seems to be a universal symbol of good in every part of the world and throughout human history."[1] How unusual is that? It's impressive and outsized, like elephants themselves.

Flights of Fact, Not Fancies

Some facts and contexts to ground euphoric fancies.

In the 1980s and 1990s, when science sent the primatologists Dian Fossey and Jane Goodall to research apes in Africa, it expected scientific results. Along with Biruté Galdikas in Indonesia, the women were expected to observe apes, identified only by numbers, and to record their activities dispassionately. They were not supposed to bond with their animal subjects. Instead, all three women fell hard for primates—Fossey for her gorillas, Goodall for her chimps, Galdikas for her orangutans. Sensing "beingness" ("humanity" would be too strong a word), the primatologists took on the godlike function of naming the creatures and told stories about ape lives and families so compellingly that these trained scientists became advocates for animal rights, claiming—as remains controversial within scientific communities, though not among most pet owners—that animals have language and respond to human speech. Science disowned the women. But popular culture took them and their subjects to its beating heart.[2] Animal rights, veganism, animal studies: in our lifetimes, we've seen a revolution in consciousness about animals.

People don't live with elephants as they do with cats and dogs, for whom familial feelings are not unusual. They don't feed them daily, like birds, fishes, and turtles. They're not working farm animals or prized athletes or hobbies, like horses. People who study elephants don't even usually live close to them, as primatologists do with apes. But in some ways, elephants align with humans more perfectly than primates do. Elephants are sexed and racy but, unlike apes, famously monogamous. Unlike gorillas, elephants don't share their females with the alpha male. Unlike chimps, they never cannibalize and are not notable for aggression. Unlike orangutans, they can be alone but are not by nature solitary. Though they're further away from humans in evolutionary terms than primates, elephants don't present the delicate problems that apes do when we try to humanize their lives. Since we don't eat elephants, we don't have to worry about that taboo either. Elephants exist not just in our minds but also in the natural world, in families.[3]

Mother elephants carry their young for a staggering twenty-two months, and infants weigh on average 260 pounds. The long gestation and hefty weight might suggest independence from birth, but that's not in fact the case. Mothers stand protectively over their babies, feeding them trunk to mouth. And because fathers keep their distance, mothers appoint surrogates, called "allomothers," who help supervise and increase the chances of the baby's survival—a tribe of Amazons and band of sisters. Like human newborns, baby elephants require and become the center of their group's attention and care.

Except in ancient warfare (Hannibal comes to mind) and in some locales (like India, where they sometimes build roads), elephants are not usually used as workers, with one notable exception. Until very recently, elephants worked and were shown at circuses, where, as children, we enjoyed ice cream and cotton candy and thrilled to the elephant parade. Our attraction to elephants began early, when we typically make less separation than adults do between animate and inanimate things, humans and beasts, and have a different sense of what belongs to our bodies and what does not. A recent bestseller by Sarah Gruen called *Water for Elephants* capitalized on how affection for elephants dates to our big-top pasts—a heritage lost now that many circuses, including the legendary Barnum and Bailey, ceased the use of elephants, and soon thereafter closed. In our nursery years, elephants' unfettered tendency toward massive pees and poops might even have impressed some of us as something like ultimate freedom.

Appropriately, then, children's books and movies often feature elephants, and, when they do, they address psychodramas that children feel acutely. Elephant moms like Dumbo's and Babar's are, for example, almost invariably goners.[4] Babar's mother gets killed matter-of-factly close to the opening of the original book: "A wicked hunter has killed Babar's mother," the first book bluntly states.[5] In deploying this motif, children's stories enact representations of loss almost as voodoo protection, a kind of cosmic knocking on wood or the symbolic enactment that Freud called *fort-da*.[6] The motif produces gratifying declarations of love and obedience from children to mothers, while allowing also first discussions of death.[7] It's curious but true that, while fairy tales often put orphan children through extended trials, granting them safety only after dangers, children's books usually quickly provide a buddy or a human guide for orphaned animals. Like other children's stories, the Babar books find the baby elephant a replacement mom — in Babar's case the Little Old Lady, who proceeds to clothe and humanize him.

On average, and once again fairly close to us, elephants live up to an average of about seventy years. They come in different physical types: Asian and African. The flat-eared and somewhat smaller Asian or Indian elephant shows up in most of the ads and images released through 1990, even though the flapping-eared larger African beast forms the huge majority of elephants worldwide, with estimates running as high as 90 percent.[8] I'm not sure why ads historically so clearly preferred Asian elephants, among whom only the males have pronounced tusks. Perhaps it happened because drawings and photos of elephants first flowed out of Asia, as did the first circus animals.

Aristotle said that elephants are beasts that "pass all others in wit and mind"; Plutarch said they have "a refinement that seems not far from human" (Scigliano, *Love, War, and Circuses*, 4): Classic philosophers loved elephants as much as we do and thought them superior creatures. Folklore features elephants who have long memories, which we associate with longevity and wisdom. In fact, the wise old elephant (usually male) remains a stock figure in folklore as common as the mother elephant. Writerly wisdom is also a primary attribute of the Indian elephant god Ganesh.

Perhaps best of all, and contributing at some level to our love of elephants, is how they communicate with one another via "infrasound" — vocalizations pitched too low for the human ear and low enough to transmit tremendous distances (Scigliano, *Love, War, and Circuses*, 3). Like apes, whales, dolphins, and other wild animals we love, they share what can be called, albeit controversially, the gift of language. In books, cartoons, and popular narratives like Tarzan, elephants understand humans, though they sometimes respond only with action. We might think of their low, unheard language as a symbol of why we love elephants. Like perfect harmony, what they say remains forever tantalizing but forever out of reach.

Described objectively by five men who are not blind, elephants would be unlovely. "Dun-colored" like mice, wrinkled and gray, with eyes set too wide apart, huge outsized noses, and gaping maws. Yet we rarely characterize or think of them that way. Instead, we feel an attraction that's not pragmatic — as it is, say, for horses, whom we ride for transportation, sport, or hobby—and not domestic either, as for cats and dogs. In the end, our attraction to elephants is more fantastical, even mythical.

Origin myths often posit a once unified field that fractured: the Big Bang; the splitting of Shiva and Shakti; Blake's time before the four Zoas; though it's partly spoiled by human control, the Garden of Eden. "At once wise and wild, enormous and delicate, monstrous and maternal," elephants reconcile opposites, Eric Scigliano suggests (*Love, War, and Circuses*, 4), producing within their massive bodies a compelling sense of oneness and nonduality. Is it too much to say that, symbolically, elephants represent some principle of stability that was once ours and that we constantly seek? When the subject is elephants, it's hard not to be rhapsodic.

And yet, despite our great and universal love for elephants, they have long been hunted for their ivory and are, today, an endangered species, more and more so as the twenty-first century advances.[9] They're endangered by us humans, who love them. And we are ourselves endangered by climate change and other disasters. As in my tale of Ellie, mortality and loss don't figure prominently in elephant facts but lurk around the edges.

Flights of Fancy

Babar's creator, Jean de Brunhoff, experienced the desolation of World War I in the trenches, but his character Babar exists within "one vast national park of fine living," like the Île-de-France, the enchanting region near Paris where de Brunhoff lived in a delightful, sun-infused manor house with his fashionable and elegant family.[10]

Babar the character was born one night when Jean's younger son Mathieu (age four) had a stomachache and the mother of the family, the glamorous and refined Cecile, told him a distracting tale. The next morning, her artistic husband "transformed Cecile's bedtime story into a book for his sons,"[11] using artists he admired as inspiration: Monet, Dufy, Pissarro, and Matisse, all of whom render lush, sunny, verdant landscapes. I note the switch from mother to father in all accounts of Babar's origins but don't want to make too much of it: Jean offered Cecile recognition as coauthor, which she refused. The de Brunhoff family, like the Babar books, kept male and female roles narrowly and, apparently, happily in place.[12] Since it was 1930 and not the twenty-first century, we perhaps should not judge that too harshly.

The first book appeared in 1930, placing Babar solidly in the Great Depression, though that reality does not appear in the tales any more than World War I does. Seven years later, Jean died young, of tuberculosis, having completed *The Travels of Babar* the previous year. By that time, the series was already so well established and well-loved in France that his elegant widow soldiered on, raising three young sons, the eldest of whom, Laurent, would have been twelve years old when his father died.

In 1946, Laurent, now twenty-one, published his own Babar book, gradually adding around twenty more over forty-five years. The books became an ongoing memorial to Jean and a legendary father-son collaboration.[13] That Babar's creator died young, and of TB, like Keats, might have made Babar the elephant a tragic symbol and sign of loss. Instead, like the books themselves, Laurent's work affirmed family continuity.

The Babar books appeared from 1930 through 1937, then lapsed until 1946: We might pause to consider all that happened during the dates that the Babar books disappeared. Munich, the invasion of Czechoslovakia and Poland, Blitzkrieg, the fall of France, Petain, collaboration and resistance, the death camps, Normandy, the liberation of Paris, the Bomb. Enormous devastation and worldwide trauma. But in Babar's world, it's always "as if there had been no death, no World War II, no interruption" (Hildebrand, *Jean and Laurent de Brunhoff*, 2). Both before and after World War II, the books exude a 1920s and early 1930s Parisian vibe.

In the 1920s, the anthropological Musée de l'Homme was much in vogue, as was Tarzan, the British lord who befriends elephants and speaks animal languages. Josephine Baker performed in Art Deco settings with a live cheetah and gorilla (Hildebrand, *Jean and Laurent de Brunhoff*, 15). Amid such primitivist extravaganzas, with their mixing and matching of decors and locales, Babar fit right in. Still, for the most part—witness the actual historical events between 1937 and 1945—Babar exists in the time warp where children's books often float, and that remains key to their appeal. The Babar books embody a family idyll where war and genocide—notable for disrupting home life—scarcely matter.[14]

Like his creators, Babar is "the quintessential gentilhomme"—a gentleman always erect on two feet once he meets humans and often garbed in a vivid green suit and black bowler hat. Visually funny, the gag of the dressed elephant makes the series work, transforming elephant hooves into hands and feet. Dressed in suits, Babar is in many ways a model consumer. He covets cars and planes, craves luxurious houses, and disdains anything as *animalistic* as a stall filled with straw, where a wicked circus owner puts him in one of the tales. In the first book, *The Story of Babar*, the purchase of clothes confirms Babar's transformation from an orphaned elephant into a gentleman. "BABAR BUYS HIMSELF [CLOTHES]," oversized script in the book proclaims. The same page itemizes lovingly each purchase—*chemises, cravats,* shirts, ties.

Babar naturally appeals to fellow consumers who buy his books. When we recall that Babar has been orphaned shortly before the spending spree, it's clear that, as for so many of us who shop and eat, "worldliness comforts him" (Weber, *The Art of Babar*, 31).

In fact, as an adult husband and king, Babar is like the perfect man on Father's Day cards: bidding farewell to his people from a balloon or contemplating the starred night sky; Babar *en voyage*—like Odysseus, one classic model for the series (Weber, *The Art of Babar*, 23); Babar-père catching butterflies or fishing. He does guy things with a gentleness and asexuality that both men and women find almost infinitely appealing. Babar is *le père de la famille*, the father of the family. But his rounded form does not seem, somehow, to exclude women, even though, or perhaps because, Babar's wife, Celeste, his daughter, and the Old Lady defer to the head male and unfailingly receive his generosity and good will. In the Babar books, as in his creator's household, Father really does know best.

Published by Hachette in France, the original Babar books were large in format, allowing for the full display of the de Brunhoffs' illustrations, with which both father and son took substantial care. They excelled at double-page formats that produced striking results, like "Babar's Return to the Forest" in *The Story of Babar* (1931). Grounded by a red sports car driven by the title character, the image features Babar's nephew Arthur (dressed in his signature white shirt and red shorts) tooting a horn on the trunk, while Celeste waves to her new kinsfolk, mostly on all fours, who flock to see the couple. The delightful image includes multiple puns on "tooting" and "trunk." As Babar drives, he tips his hat to his clan, like a cup held by a menagerie elephant. The car and its human-like occupants, surrounded by the more realistic-looking elephant herd: in their illustrations, the Babar books effortlessly bridge the human and animal worlds.

In the late 1950s, Hachette reduced the Babar books' format, which required some deletions.[15] Soon after that, Random House picked up the series, and Babar came to America. The first Random House books used boldface type; Jean had used handwritten script. They printed key words in French, colored blue, and English, colored black (Weber, *The Art of Babar*, 133). In 1963, the American giant became Babar's primary publisher.

I might have encountered Babar at this point, except that my family had no connection to France or to things French—and so I didn't. My primary symbolic connection to elephants was Ellie. I've got to admit, if it has not already shown, that despite my love for Ellie, I didn't read Babar as a child. Few American children of my generation did.

Though hugely popular in his native land and available in a 1950 Random

House paperback, Babar "was not exactly a household word [in America] . . . before the 1960s" (Hildebrand, *Jean and Laurent de Brunhoff*, 67). By the time Babar fully arrived, I was emerging from childhood into the charged milieu of the Kennedy and King assassinations and a political world in tumult. Because we tend to read our children the things we read when we were young, I didn't read Babar to my daughters either. I read Dr. Dolittle instead, a character with clear and definite affinities to Babar.

Dr. Dolittle has a short, rounded shape—full and elephantine—in ayurvedic terms, a *kapha* body that loves stillness, good food, and comfort.[16] He talks to the animals, and they talk to him, bridging (as Babar does), humanity and beasts. Dolittle and his animals are other reasons why, I think, I always seem to have had a thing for Babar merchandise (postcards, stuffed dolls), before I actually read the books. Babar's image is charming, bright, and fun.[17] In every line of his face and body, he radiates the same expressive bonhomie as Dr. Dolittle, a character I loved so much that I kept the first book I borrowed from the library long enough to incur serious fines, which made my parents threaten to revoke my library card, though they didn't.

Like Babar's author, Dolittle's creator, Hugh Lofting, experienced World War I—in fact, he sent the original stories home to his children from the trenches—but did not draw on that event in the Dolittle stories. Instead, again like Babar, Dr. Dolittle exists in a timeless wonderland that links adults to children's worlds of imagination and play. Read in the family, often a middle class or aspiring one, both Dolittle and Babar allow us to love animals and the utter goodness that Babar and Dolittle represent. They also allow us to love and appreciate the material world that supports our home.[18] The books don't urge us to sacrifice or to live austerely, like Saint Francis or Dian Fossey, who also loved and championed beasts. Instead, we exist in the same mix-and-match never-never-lands as Babar and Dolittle, who can quickly solve dilemmas in the social world, even (for the most part), sensitive issues like race.[19] Like my elephant statues and pillows, and like my Ellie herself, the inexpensive books are merchandise. But in the sense of lightness and joy they give, they're magical and priceless.

In his journal *Household Words*, the Victorian novelist Charles Dickens posited our need for fantasy and play and the family's ability to nourish both, as an alternative to what he called the workplace's "whirling wheel of toil."[20] He filled his novels with characters and families that are utilitarian and grim, like Uriah Heap, Gradgrind, the Smallweeds, Lord and Lady Dedlock, whose names tell the tale. But Dickens loved characters who live life inventively as play, giving everyday existence extraordinary grace: David and Barkis in *David Copperfield*, teasing Bella and her Pa in *Our Mutual Friend*, Joe and even

Magwitch in *Great Expectations*. In my married family and with my children, I've learned that life is better rounded—playful, funny, and jolly.

Ganesh Is My Guy

With a human body but an elephant head, Ganesh is a personified elephant god, but something more—in his case, much more. He's the writer's god and also the god of ideas and wisdom. Removing obstacles and nurturing new beginnings, Ganesh stands quite naturally at the entrances to Indian temples and gets invoked whenever a new project, business, or journey begins. Once I got seriously into yoga, Ganesh began to focus my collection of elephants and to surpass my representations of the natural beasts. Elephant of elephants, my guy of guys, Ganesh returns us to the question of why we love elephants one more time, in classic myths about family and mortality.

In Hindu mythology, Ganesh's father is Shiva—the male principle and one of Hinduism's three major deities, who is by turns the Devourer and a dancing, lingam god. Ganesh's mother, Parvati, forms one of two incarnations of Shiva's female spouse. The first incarnation, Sati, lives ascetically, but asceticism doesn't have much to do with Ganesh. The second incarnation of Shiva's bride, Ganesh's mother, Parvati, represents lightheartedness and the perfect wife and mother. Shiva tests Parvati by berating himself while disguised as a "Brahmin of short stature."[21] It's the kind of test perfect wives often face in myth and legend: Think of Penelope in the *Odyssey* and Chaucer's patient Griselda. He asks Parvati if she knows that Shiva is "an ugly, homeless mendicant of dirty habits, a haunter of cemeteries and an ill-tempered old god besides" (Johnson and Johnson, *God and Gods in Hinduism*, 73). Parvati closes her ears at the blasphemy and shouts at the Brahmin until he reveals himself as smiling, hunky Shiva, pleased at his wife's loyalty. Testing the wife is a classic motif; so too is the beggar-like disguise (remember the *Odyssey*), followed by a sexy reunion.

Unlike Shiva and his wife, who both have dual identities, Ganesh has only one incarnation, which is always peaceful and calm. Never married, Ganesh remains a unitary, solo god, accompanied only (and quite comically) by the tiny rat on whom he travels, encompassing, as elephants do, the reconciliation of opposites.

Ganesh has a fat rounded body topped by a huge, outsized elephant's head. Unlike his mother and father, he's not beautiful. He's weird looking and potentially a monster, though he is understood immediately to be both sweet and loveable. He might be all the way to scary except—as cartoonists have known for centuries—Ganesh's proportions are universally appealing and *cute*. His outsized head suggests human babies, seal pups, puppies, and kittens. We want to take him to our hearts as closely as I must have held Ellie to wear her velvet so thin and smooth. In fact, it's possible to own a baby Ganesh—a small, reclining figure that makes absolutely clear the link between Ganesh and infants.

Legend has it that Ganesh got his head when his mother Parvati took a bath and told her son to guard the door, turning away all visitors. Barred entry by his son and in a wrathful, devouring mood, Shiva struck off Ganesh's head. The myth holds the potential for stressing tragedy and death, not to mention Freudian themes. You don't have to be a psychoanalyst to read the elements in this myth as a classic family romance—the bath, the son as guard, the two-faced father, a rivalry, a symbolic castration. Except that, seeing Parvati's tears and being divine, Shiva repents and promises to mend the situation by using the head of the next being that passes to make her son whole. The next being was an elephant, and so, with the sublime incoherence of myth and legend, Parvati got her son back in the form of a demi-elephant, and Ganesh's rounded jolliness defuses the tale. Like Babar and Dolittle, Ganesh inclines toward happiness.

Usually posed upright, either seated or on his toes, Ganesh statues often wave multiple arms, but they do not suggest the potential violence or devastation of a Shiva or a Kali, the multilimbed creation-destruction principle, who is usually portrayed inside a wheel. Instead, Ganesh wields a pen or a brush in one hand or holds a globe that looks like an acorn or chalice. With the other, he flashes the outward palm of peace.[22] In Ganesh's legends, as in so many elements of elephant lore, death and mortality hover but they do not dominate the tale.

For those who know India only slightly, as I do, the place is both a marvel of sights and colors and a bit confusing. The books *Holy Cow* and *Jeff in Venice/Death in Varanasi* capture some of the conflicting emotions I felt when I went there the year after my mother died—the second of my yoga journeys during a time of grief.[23] Everywhere you go in India, it's possible to see great beauty and great poverty side by side. Statues—sometimes Hanuman, the monkey god, but more often Ganesh—are laden with flowers and ringed with honorific garlands. Famously, India is filled with contradictions: allusions to death often draped in riotous colors.

One day, I was driving in Thiruvananthapuram, the capital city of Kerala— Conrad's Malabar, and the region where one of my favorite contemporary classics, Arundhati Roy's *The God of Small Things*, takes place. All morning I had been seeing posters of Ganesh and marveling at their diversity and charm. Then, to my left and to my surprise, I saw a large open doorway and what looked like a Disneyland of white, unpainted Ganeshas of all sizes—hundreds of them. Thinking it too good to be true, I stopped the cab, got out, and found myself surrounded by children-sized Ganeshas, adult-sized Ganeshas, and giant Ganeshas towering above me. I shook their hands. I took pictures. I wandered freely all around in the way that India lets you wander without asking questions. I wanted to see the Ganeshas, I wanted to be with the Ganeshas. Though they were unpainted and (I was told) not yet done, I got the chance.

It was the eve of Chaturthi, a major holiday in which multiple Ganeshas get paraded through the streets by candlelight amid much merriment and then eased, en masse, into the river, where their plaster dissolves. "In towns and villages, they carry your images in procession," a prayer runs. "There is laughter in the home and out in the streets. But there is also sadness when we cast away your images, when we immerse them in the sea. When we depart, we hear the waves mutter your name" (Johnson and Johnson, *God and Gods in Hinduism*, 82). *We cast away your images, but the waves utter your name*: It seems only fitting that Ganesh's chief ritual echoes with far more serious stories around the world in which a god appears only to be destroyed.[24]

On Chaturthi, in the lightest and most playful of moods, multiple statues of Ganesh dissolve, merging into totality, like the classic grain of sand on a beach or drop of salt in the ocean. Nestled in the Ganesh story—as in Babar's narrative, in our love for elephants, and in my tale of Ellie—mortality asserts itself, but gently, without a mournful tune. Matter becomes element, without protest and with joy.[25] There's a peacefulness here, a flow I find quite perfect.

Ganesh, the most solid and fleshly of gods, surrenders his form annually in a friendly group ritual. The action takes us back to the core reason we love elephants.

Dissolution hovers. But while it's ours, life should be enjoyed on our own, in our families, with our friends. Warm and full and jolly.

PART III
Memory without Pain

7
Food as Anthropological Lens

If we close our eyes and remember the food or dish we associate most with family and with home, what do we see? Apple pie or *apfelkuchen*? Black-eyed peas and collards? Corned beef and cabbage? Roasted chicken with potatoes? Bagels and lox? Ramen or *pho*? Pasta with gravy? Grilled steak or roast beef? The answer varies by where our ancestors came from and how much tradition fueled the cooking in our households. Food focuses an anthropological lens on generations, communities, and cultures, bringing us back to the Ilongot tribe with which we began in the Introduction, who recite the names of places they have gardened in times of grief.

Within anthropology, food studies considers a group's reliance on a single staple or its large, overall patterns, including gender roles in food production. The field examines, for example, the economic implications of rice in Asian cultures, of cassava in many African ones, of potatoes for Ireland and Eastern Europe, and also food's role in migration patterns. It links food to whole sets of histories, values, and practices.[1]

While food studies as a field may be fairly new, anthropology's attention goes back further, at least to the landmark work of Claude Lévi-Strauss in *The Raw and the Cooked* (1954).[2] I remember an aging Lévi-Strauss speaking at Columbia University, decades after this book appeared, to an excited, overflow crowd wanting to learn more about structuralism, an approach that links phenomena from everyday life to myth and philosophical theory. Small and compact, but extremely elegant, Lévi-Strauss spoke for more than three hours, and, though I grew restless like the rest of the crowd, I loved how he connected a culture's attitudes toward food to whole sets of paired values: the moist and the dry, the fresh and the rotten, and, ultimately, the living and the dead. Suitably, given its multiple implications, food figures into many mourning rituals, marking not just liminality but also permeability between those who survive and those who pass. It's no wonder, then, that memoirs of loss sometimes mention food and even, like this one, include recipes.

A landmark 2012 production of Thornton Wilder's *Our Town*, directed by David Cromer, made the point powerfully. In the play, the young heroine Emily, who has died in childbirth, has been given the chance to revisit "home" on one day of her choosing; at the end of act 1, she chooses the morning of her twelfth birthday. As the audience reentered the theater after intermission, noses began to twitch as our senses registered not just the sight of coffee brewing and someone putting bacon in a pan (which would be ordinary) but also the *smell* of coffee and bacon permeating the theater from a section that had been curtained off during the first half of the play. Kitchen. Home. Family. Revealed and embodied in the olfactory memory of food.

Family recipes allow a son or daughter to recreate and reenact a parent's cooking. And so, as I mourned my mother and wrote *Crossing Back*, my mother's recipes served as a beacon, leading the way to memory without pain. Alongside reading, meditating, and writing, her recipes—all Italian-American classics—were bases I needed to touch after my birth family's death.

I am not the first or only Italian-American woman to write about food. Many famous Italian-American females have published cookbooks as tributes to our rich food histories. Other literary critics have written about food too, among them Louise DeSalvo in *Crazy in the Kitchen*, where she introduces profound generational dislikes. DeSalvo describes her family's general food ambiance as follows:

> The people in our house behaved like characters in an opera or in a tragedy (Greek, not Shakespearean).
> In our house, a dish broken by accident, an oversalted gravy, some spilled oil, a messy floor, an annoying child, a late library book, a dirty dress, a missed curfew was never a problem or a challenge. In our house, everything was a *very big deal*, an occasion for high drama.
> In our house, no one ever went with the flow. There was no flow. There were only dangerous rapids, huge whirlpools, gigantic waterfalls. In our house, you had to be very vigilant. To stop paying attention, even for a moment, was dangerous.[3]

While I compare certain attitudes and moments in my family to Greek tragedy—DeSalvo and I both having been educated in the classics—I could never write these sentences, or, if I did, I would be lying. In my childhood home, things were very orderly, the floors and kitchen were always spotless, food was always surrounded by the aura of generational love, and I am hard-pressed to remember very many scenes of yelling or screaming or wrath. My paternal grandmother Marianna De Marco (after whom I am named) died before I was born and added a Sicilian touch to my mother's Calabrese cooking, which my mother always acknowledged fondly. Unlike DeSalvo as a girl, I always ate my mother's food, which, unlike her mother's, was authentically delicious and definitely a way she showed her love. My childhood food memories resemble Andrew Cuomo's euphoric descriptions, during his COVID-19 briefings, of peaceable weekly gatherings of grandparents, parents, siblings, and cousins over midday Sunday dinner.

Because it was a fulcrum of family memory, I gathered all the recipes I had for my daughters into a bound notebook, forming an archive of memory we could all access at will. When I did, certain recipes immediately signified the plenitude of home: for example, meat sauce, also called "gravy," and its constituent meatballs. Successfully executed, they allowed me—someone with good food instincts but by no means an accomplished chef—to step into my mother's favorite medium of creativity, which was cooking, and to enact the generational continuity I craved.

Other recipes in the notebook produced more anxiety or, at least, a sense of challenge because they demanded steps that must be done just right—and I was not at all sure I could do them. For me, the tricky dishes were lasagna, eggplant parmigiana, and cream puffs.

Just as Lévi-Strauss would predict, all these recipes embody certain deep principles of Italian and Italian-American culture that I already knew but felt in a poignant, bodily way while cooking. In fact, and I am not stretching it here, my mother's recipes seemed like metaphors for important Italian-American values like *control* and *relationship*. *Control* in the sense of taking the time to do things right and the native tendency toward decorum and keeping an eye on the eyes of others—looking good in front of the neighbors or the community at large. *Relationship* in terms of things that belong together staying together, with special emphasis on what I'll call "bonding" and "layering" as ways of combining things without obliterating differences. Bonding and layering seemed like perfect metaphors for the way that Italian families remain strong, even though people quarrel, or marry, and sometimes move away. Food signifies my family themes and especially their shifting dynamics.

But, ultimately, for me—and I suspect for many others—there are foods and recipes that signify a loved one's loss, perhaps because the food was eaten close to that person's death, or served at the funeral meal, or because the recipe no longer exists and cannot be recreated. My missing link and, therefore, the only piece that could really complete my puzzle was the recipe for a pastry called sfingi that went missing. Missing. Like my stuffed elephant Ellie, like my family photographs, like my mother herself. I end this chapter on the power of food as an anthropological lens with the story of sfingi, making connections along the way between the art of cooking and the experience of writing this book.

Recipe 1: Meat Sauce (Gravy)

Foundational. That's what meat sauce, also known as red sauce, Bolognese, "sugo," or "gravy" is to most Italian-American households.[4] Foundational and basic. If one serves just the meat, it's a dish on its own, but it's usually served with pasta. It also forms a building block for many other dishes. The directions I give here come verbatim from my mother.

Meat Sauce (Gravy)

> Brown meat, cut onion, and garlic (add garlic last) (Vegetables like mushrooms or eggplant can be used instead of meat but won't be as good.)
> Take a can of tomato paste and stir into the pot
> Open a large can of plum tomatoes, chop, and add to the pot
> Add a little sugar (¼ tsp)
> Bay leaf, parsley, and basil are optional
> Salt and pepper to taste

My mother made excellent meat sauce: rich, savory, and balanced, with a southern Italian spin borrowed from my Sicilian grandmother. Surviving cousins frequently praise it, saying—and it's a form of heresy, in a way—that their own mothers' gravy paled by comparison. In one case, a Neapolitan in-law's sauce was always so greasy that, when we went to visit, my mother would pack roast beef sandwiches for the family to eat on the bus to New Jersey so that we could nibble just enough pasta with gravy to be polite. I remember my mother tutoring my aunt about the need to skim her gravy as the meat cooked or to use leaner cuts, seemingly to little effect. My aunt's gravy was, no doubt, a family legacy of her own.

My mother's sauce was excellent but would be difficult for most people, including me, to reproduce precisely from the recipe she gave. I want to shout across the wedge of time: How much meat and onion and garlic, Ma? Just lightly brown the meat, or make it dark? And how long should I cook the sauce? For, like many recipes my mother gave me or left behind, the recipe for sauce leaves out quantities and timing, which she, as a well-practiced cook, rarely measured.

I do know certain things. I know the standard small can of tomato paste she means, maybe two inches round; I know, by color, the exact large can of plum tomatoes she preferred, although I also know she bought cheaper when she could. The pinch of sugar is an Italian secret gone public and the folkloric reason why authentic sauce is sometimes called "sugo." I even know the meats I should brown, vegetables being listed only because, to my mother's dismay, my older daughter is a vegetarian.

For the best gravy, you use some pork (chunks but especially plump sausage links both hot and sweet), some beef (chunks or, better still, a braciola, a thin steak pounded flat and stuffed with cheese, parsley and garlic, then rolled and tied with string), and some meatballs, a recipe on their own. When feeling decadent, you can substitute a pork braciola for the beef, using a piece of fatty skin that can also bind a dynamite minestra (soup).

My mother may have left out cooking times to show confidence in my instincts as a chef but really, I suspect, because she didn't want to discourage me. I tend to cook a meal in thirty minutes or less—to reach for the Pomi, toss in the seasonings, and heat the sauce only as long as it takes to boil the pasta. But sauce should cook slowly, for an hour and a half at least and more likely two or two and a half—its rich savory smell permeating the home and making the stove the equivalent of the family hearth. You can't just turn on the burner and leave it: You have to skim frequently to remove the fat and adjust the seasonings.

Italians and Italian-Americans could write a book, or certainly a longer disquisition, on the subject of meat sauce, red sauce, Bolognese, or "gravy" and its many other names. But for me, metaphor beckons. Let's call loss and mourning the foundation of this book: the loss of my mother, followed by my brother. That's the meat. It could be left full of raw emotion, freeform, relatively unprocessed—at its worst all the way to whiney. That kind of writing is not for me, even though, when they're done well, grief memoirs can be very fine.

Like the tomatoes in the sauce, great books form an essential ingredient in *Crossing Back* since they cook the meat. At first, my losses being quotidian and my lacking celebrity, I thought recourse to great books would justify a memoir about my mother's and brother's deaths. But by the time the sauce was cooked (the book was done), I realized that books were not just an occasion and a justification. Great literature raises family matters to mythic levels that touch us all; it enacts patterns we might recognize around our Thanksgiving tables. Reading and writing about books encouraged me to excavate core emotions; they taught me that my emotions after my mother's death reached further back, even much further back than I'd thought.

Reviewing and then enacting the recipe for sauce taught me that it was okay to slow things down. For loss to be accepted, my book needed to simmer a good long while, as the gravy did in that big pot of my mother that's mine now.

Recipe 2: Meatballs

While simple, the recipe for meatballs takes two radically different kinds of ingredients and makes them into a whole. On one side, chopped meat; on the other, eggs, breadcrumbs, cheese, and garlic, with water lubricating the mix. While my mother used only top-quality beef, cajoling the local butcher to sell her the best sirloin and rejecting anything inferior, then watching closely as he ground it to order, it's possible to add or substitute veal, pork, or lamb.

My Mother's Meatballs

Take 1 lb. chopped meat (high quality best)
Add 2 eggs, ½ cup breadcrumbs, a handful of cheese, 1 clove of
    minced garlic, parsley, salt, and pepper
Mix, adding water (up to ¼ cup) to make moist
Shape into balls (for sauce) or small thick patties
Boil the balls in sauce or fry the patties

Delicious in sauce and, like sauce, a building block for other recipes, boiled meatballs are soft and tender, meeting all the requirements of classic comfort food, including a mother's love. They're excellent when served with the cliché spaghetti or more southern Italian–style rigatoni. They're also delicious in a roll or in a hero. Perhaps best of all, but rare in the United States, are fried meatballs: Far tastier than hamburger and more complex, they can be eaten on their own or, like the American standard, served with ketchup. If you like Japanese cuisine, it fries chopped beef with a flavor that's reminiscent of my mother's fried meatballs. Adding pine nuts, Middle Eastern cuisine offers kibbeh.

Like the mixtures in this recipe for meatballs, my book mixes memories of my mother and my brother over time, because his love for her and hers for him always colored my relationships to both. My feelings toward my mother stayed fairly constant over my life—respect, admiration, love, but also wariness—changing as our lives proceeded and she moved from being the mother I saw every day to the mother I spoke to by phone.

My feelings toward my brother changed radically between childhood and adulthood, so that a food with a hole at the center (a doughnut, an Indian poori, a cream puff shell, only the last being a family recipe) would be an apt metaphor too. But when all is said and done, there was a solidity in my bond with my brother, a connection at the core that the mixed- and mashed-up meatball—made by hand and rounded in shape—captures best. Despite our differences, and there were many, we were our parents' children, both for better and for worse. Capable, smart, efficient, usually quite reliable—but sometimes lacking (as canny peasants often do) empathy and fellow feeling.

My mother's meatball recipe offers a model for how I wanted this memoir to turn out: a mixture of two separate things—memoir and criticism—that coheres into a rounded whole. But I couldn't get there until I learned to layer.

Recipe 3: Lasagna

Making lasagna assumes that certain other things have already been done. The sauce needs to be complete and ready to hand, along with the extra meatballs and sausage you'll mash and add back to the sauce. The large flat ribbons of pasta used for the dish, always liable to stick or break, must be boiled to perfection and carefully drained. Oil can help prevent the sticking but cannot remedy a fatal mistake like undercooked or overcooked pasta. Most of all, lasagna is all about layering: sauce, pasta, and the ricotta mixture—one layer over another, with not too much of any one layer, and not too little.

Rose Cozzitorto De Marco's Lasagna

Make sauce with extra meatballs and sausage
Boil lasagna in salted water until tender (¾ lb); a bit of oil prevents sticking
Chop a small mozzarella
Mash meatballs and sausage and add back to sauce
Strain pasta, being careful, but making it nice and dry
Mix 1 lb. ricotta, 2 eggs, the chopped mozzarella, some parmesan cheese (not too thick and not too watery)
Put a layer of sauce in a rectangular pan
Layer pasta and ricotta mixture, ending with sauce at the top
Bake until the sauce is bubbly and the lasagna is done
Let it sit a little before cutting and serving

Lasagna requires repeated careful judgments: the ratio of filling to pasta, for example, makes one lasagna memorable but another too wet or too dry or not savory or sweet enough. My mother's lasagna was always perfect, though I remember seeing her perform emergency measures on the rare occasions it was not, like draining off excess water before serving.

There are Italian restaurants called Lasagna (are they kidding?). And, sometimes, like bad Italian joints, we overbake or reheat lasagna carelessly. But a dismissive attitude of any kind is a mistake. Lasagna requires time and care to assemble, and so much can go wrong—including that ricotta mixture, which has to be, as my mother says, not too thick and not too watery. Like basic sauce, lasagna makes for a work-intensive dish; if you count the time it takes to make the sauce and the meatballs, then that much more. But even with a premade sauce, lasagna needs to cook until it's done, usually for sixty to ninety minutes. And then it needs to sit just long enough. Only then is it ready to cut into pieces and eat.

Like sauce and meatballs, lasagna is well known in Italy and America as comfort food. It tends to be the kind of thing we take for granted because we use it to feed a crowd. But, properly conceived, lasagna has a grandeur about it—the sense of being a project. I wouldn't want to lose the flourish, the blare of a herald's trumpet, that should accompany lasagna.

It's a tricky recipe for a chef and offers an apt metaphor for a writer. Are all the materials at hand worthy of combining? Put together, will they make the right dish—or will it be too watery (sentimental) or too dry (inaccessible)? Most of all, as a metaphor, lasagna is about layering, each layer getting covered by the next in order to finish the dish. As I wrote *Crossing Back*, I learned that I had covered some memories up in the past. Have I revealed them in a way that makes sense and preserves their integrity? Have I betrayed anyone I love in doing so?

Recipe 4: Eggplant Parmigiana

Like lasagna, eggplant parmigiana is inexpensive peasant food. But, also like lasagna, eggplant parm is work intensive and complicated. It's not like classic French cuisine, with many fine-tuned maneuvers. But it's complicated nonetheless. You have to slice the eggplant the proper thickness and give it time to drain (my mother's touch). You have to coat it carefully, making sure the breadcrumb mix adheres. You have to bake (another of her touches, to make it lighter) or fry the breaded eggplant. All that done, you still have to assemble the whole—layering once again a theme—and then to bake the dish for sixty to ninety minutes, until bubbly. You have to cool it. Do all this, and you'll have a dish that tastes great hot and tastes even better reheated the next day or in sandwiches.

Rose De Marco's Eggplant Parmigiana

Slice eggplant ¼ to ½ inch thick

Sprinkle with salt and squeeze with a paper towel to take out the extra water

While the eggplant sits in the salt, prepare a breadcrumb mixture, with parsley, salt, and pepper, and optional minced garlic, grated parmesan cheese, or basil

Dip each slice in the egg and then coat with the breadcrumb mixture, patting down to firm its sticking to the eggplant

Bake on a greased cookie sheet *or* fry and drain well

Slice a small mozzarella in half or quarters and slice each part thinly

Have a favorite tomato sauce ready (gravy or canned, if necessary)

Layer eggplant, sauce, mozzarella in a baking pan: square or small rectangular pan is ideal, round okay too

Bake in a 350-degree oven until bubbly, cool a bit, slice, and serve

I see a lot of give and take in the way my mother transmitted her recipe for eggplant parmigiana. She wanted to make sure I did things right, for instance, in breading and crisping the eggplant. She made a major concession about using a commercial tomato sauce rather than my own gravy. I also sense that she wanted to cut me some slack on the shape of the pan, knowing I wouldn't have that many choices.

Near where I live in Manhattan, there was a tiny restaurant (now a chain) that, by day, served sandwiches and the basic Italian appetizers my mother also made—fried red peppers paired with a mound of fresh ricotta, that kind of thing. (I use the past tense in this paragraph because, in becoming a chain, the restaurant lost some of its allure.) Its specialty was eggplant parmigiana, plated or on a loaf. The place was always crowded, the patrons in a mood that verged on frenzy. People who had driven in from Jersey or Staten Island just couldn't wait to get that eggplant parm, those peppers. They oohed, they ah-ed, they marveled. They hovered over other tables while waiting their turn. Once, a couple at the next table was even named (I swear) Tony and Carmela, *Sopranos*-style, and quite vocally from New Jersey. Eggplant parmigiana inspires strong feelings. Associated with mothers or nonnas, it's almost sacred.

My husband's favorite dish is eggplant parmigiana. Asked what he'd like to eat the next day, he'll almost always say eggplant parmigiana. And he's not even Italian. But he knows and I know two things: Even when the eggplant is baked, not fried, eggplant parmigiana is a fattening dish, and it takes a lot of time to prepare, time I don't usually have. I try to buy versions instead of making them, though they are rarely (even that tiny restaurant's) as good as my mother's. On special occasions, very special, I make my mama's true, my mama's original and signature eggplant parmigiana. That's appropriate in its way, since, without my mother, I might not have married Stu, and the marriage has been a happy thing in my life. Like making eggplant parm, writing takes time. Like cooking, life's best when savory for the long term.

Recipe 5: Cream Puffs—Shells and Cream

The recipe for cream puffs comes in two parts, one savory and one sweet. They're both demanding recipes, the savory perhaps even more than the sweet. Most good recipes, and certainly most good meals, balance savory and sweet flavors all the time. Savory is often the harder, more mature taste because it can sometimes be salty, even bitter. Sweetness takes us back to childhood and, if our childhoods have been happy, or at least good enough, memory tastes no worse than bittersweet. Balancing savory and sweet, with the proper patience and control, the recipe produces a triumph of a dessert.

The De Marco Cream Puffs

The Shells:

> ½ cup Crisco, melted in a sauce pan (2 tbs from can; measure for ½ cup when it's melted)
> Add 1 cup of water to the pan and a pinch of salt; boil
> Add 1 cup of flour, stirring to smooth
> Add 4 eggs (2 at a time); stir with egg beater or spoon or mixer until smooth
> Grease baking pan and spoon, 1 tsp at a time (5 across)
> Bake 30 minutes at 350 degrees until golden
> Don't open the oven until done!

The Filling / Cream (Crème Anglaise)

> Take 2 cups of milk
> In one cup of milk, put 6–7 level tbs of flour and beat until smooth
> Then add the second cup of milk
> Add 2 egg yolks, ½ cup of sugar, 1 tsp vanilla extract
> Cool and stir over a low flame until it thickens; shut off heat
> Keep cooling, stirring in bowl to prevent a crust from forming
> When halfway cool, put in refrigerator, covered with Saran Wrap (It's okay to make the cream the night before the pastries)

When the pastries are cool, slit and fill with 1 tsp of cream
Sprinkle with powdered sugar

Even on the page, these are complicated recipes, filled with pitfalls: "prevent a crust from forming," mix "until smooth." The recipe for shells includes, as a simple fact, an outright warning: "Don't open the oven until done!" or everything will collapse. When baking cream puff shells, if you open up too soon, you'll end up with flat shells that are gooey and (if baked just long enough) delicious on their own when warm but no longer suitable for stuffing. And yet opening the oven is, obviously, a risk that has to be taken. Baked properly, cream puff shells will be moist but firm and provide a place for the sweet filling.

Shells pose a lot of challenges even before you bake them. The cream puff dough gets stirred, for example, with an egg beater, spoon, or mixer until smooth. As I transcribed the recipe, I felt my mother making accommodations for my more limited kitchens, only one of which has a mixer. But there were some accommodations she wouldn't make: The recipe includes Crisco, for instance, which feels archaic and certainly not healthy. And, finally, though the recipe reads easily and may seem simple, I can assure you that if the texture of the dough is wrong—if you use four eggs, say, but needed only two—you're done here, because the result will be too soft. And if you open the oven door too soon . . . well, as I've said, then you are really done.

My mother's cream, a variation on crème anglaise (a term she would not have known), is delicious. It has some pitfalls, chiefly a failure of texture, which makes it lumpy or either too thick or too thin. But stirred carefully and with love, the taste and texture delight the taste buds. When I order a Cuban *tres leches* cake or a French *oeufs à la neige* (a floating island), I always ask for extra crème anglaise, of which I can't get enough, a taste that reminds me of my mother. That said, my mother's cream puff cream can't be as liquid as a crème anglaise. It has to thicken to be used in cream puffs, but not (as my Mom says, quite clearly) too much.

Like the maker of cream puffs, writers also put together savory and sweet ingredients and themes, mixing and mingling with care. Especially in memory work, you don't want the result to be too savory—which can translate, for writing, as boring or off-putting, academic or jargony. You also don't want it to be too sweet—for writing, overly sentimental or whiney. We want it to be just right, by which I mean clear enough to hang together but surprising enough to hold a reader's interest. Like a meal, *Crossing Back* has moved, in the progression of its chapters, from the bitterest savory toward sweetness. I have to hope that the mix pleases, as my mother's finished cream puffs did.

Recipe 6: Sfingi

Bombolini, zeppole, sfingi, churros, fry bread, krullers: Even within Italy, they go by different names, their texture varying from smooth to coarse to crumbly, their flavor from almost savory to sweet. But any way you cut it—round and regular or fried in the shape that hits the pan—they're basic comfort food. Fried dough, cheap to make but also tricky, even treacherous.

Rose's Sfingi

1 lb. ricotta (Polly-O best)
2 eggs (maybe 3?)
½ cup sugar
1½ tsp. baking powder
2 cups of flour (1½ at first)
Mix with hands or mixer; it will be a soft dough—but not too soft
Spoon into a deep pot filled halfway with hot oil (it is hot enough
    when a drop of water sizzles off quickly)
Brown evenly over medium heat
Drain and cool
Sprinkle with powdered sugar
Yum [That's an added comment]

Like memory work, the sfingi recipe presents from the start certain challenges. The dough used must be soft, my mother says, but not too soft, an error akin to too much sweetness. Trial and error shows that dough with too few eggs won't be soft enough and will produce sfingi coarser in texture than my mom's, more like a Neapolitan zeppole than her Sicilian (via my paternal grandmother) brand. Zeppole are delicious when wrapped with prosciutto and eaten by hand. But they're not sfingi.

The number of eggs remains key and forms, as eggs often do, a matter of judgment. Unless you're working with jumbo eggs, three or even four is what you want, even without that extra half cup of flour. Ultimately, three or four remains a matter of judgment. As with cream puff shells, you want the result not too soft but not too hard either. You want it to be just right.

I shadowed and wrote down my mother's recipe for sfingi some years before she died, making them on Christmas Eve at midnight along with a traditional coil of thin and utterly delicious pork sausage. The pairing dates back to the days when Catholics abstained from meat on Christmas Eve: We'd feel so deprived, or so the pretense went, that we would be longing for it by midnight.

And once meat was on the table, why not some kind of fried dough not quite like cake but not quite like bread either, since it would be late and way past dinner or dessert? Voila! Coiled sausage and fried sfingi as a custom—rustic in the extreme. No one I know really feels hungry after the seafood extravaganza that goes by the name "Feast of the Seven Fishes." But the late-night snack serves as a pretty custom and a lovely fiction.

I made sfingis every year until, during one of my several unsettling moves around the time my mother died, the recipe got lost. Lost. Which would have been no big deal except that, by the time I realized it, my mother was dead and her recipe book was missing—like the family photos and the ring, whose losses I have recorded in this book. Loss upon loss, with my mother and brother irreplaceable and the recipes, while far smaller, irreplaceable too.

A moment of silence, therefore, for some recipes I had not transcribed in my mother's kitchen: her handmade ravioli, laid out on her bed, on a table-cloth, before cooking; her dense dried sausage-, egg-, and cheese-laden Easter pie, for which pizza rustica is a poor substitute; the soft but fried Christmas wine cookies drenched in honey and covered with sprinkles I used to scorn but would love, now, to taste. Scrawled in my father's hand, my mother's small, black, rectangular recipe book was something we had all seen and could picture. But after she died, we just couldn't find it, limiting me to just the handful of recipes I'd previously transcribed.

My mother went into the hospital right before Thanksgiving and died in a hospice shortly before Christmas. My best guess is that she brought the recipe notebook with her, just in case the holidays found her still bedbound. If so, she too would have considered her recipes a legacy, to be executed by me. Appropriately, then, the sfingi recipe came to symbolize loss, my mother's loss, traditions lost, the slipperiness of the past, and the difficulty of crossing back.

Then, after I had given up all hope and had already compiled a notebook for my daughters to preserve the recipes I *did* have, the phone rang. It was my younger daughter. "Mom!" she said, her voice filled with excitement. "I've got it! I found it! I thought you'd sent it to me, and I have it—the recipe for sfingi!" Later that night, I found as well an e-mail, trumpeting "I FOUND THE SFINGI RECIPE!!!!"—a heading a little like WORLD WAR II ENDS IN EUROPE!!!! My daughter added a "Yum"—which I have adopted as my own.

Sfingis represent, then, a Proustian moment of time regained, a perfect now-ness like, and in fact very like, the taste of Proust's mother's madeleine at the end of the first volume of À *la recherche du temps perdu*. A moment of perfect love, balance, and fulfillment, encased in luscious fried dough.

8

Real Estate / Unreal Estate

Selling the House

Not a ghost, not a vision, there he was: my father at age sixty-nine, though he died at eighty, standing in the living room of my Durham house and looking around at its cathedral ceilings, just as he had the day we moved in. Saying, as he had more than twenty years earlier, "This is the kind of house you see in movies. The kind of house rich people live in. Congratulations, Marianna."

Back then, my parents had driven with us to North Carolina to babysit while we closed on the house. Now, crossing from the foyer to the living room, I was filled with thoughts of family—moving in, births and birthdays, holidays when my parents had joined us. So, there he was: my father, who has been dead since the end of 1992. Not a ghost, not a vision, simply there but also not there—a memory as vivid as a hologram. A presence summoned up by my decision to sell the house but also by my being madly and irrationally reluctant to do so.

How do you sell a house when you have an instinct for places you've been happy, a variation on what Italians call the *sta casa* gene? Furtively, and with considerable angst that will lead, I learn over time, to a peculiar desire to possess, all at once, all the places I have ever lived. Rich in metaphor, fraught with meaning, what does it mean, finally, to sell the house?

My parents married on July 4, 1943, an all-American gesture, since their engagement party had taken place on December 7, 1941, the day Japan bombed Pearl Harbor. Independence Day might have been chosen by my mother ironically because marriage released her, as the unmarried daughter in an Italian family, from becoming caretaker to her parents as they aged. The apartment my parents moved into that July 4 became the only place they ever lived as a couple. Small, even by New York standards, it had only three nine-by-twelve rooms in addition to a larger eat-in kitchen.

Curtains and bedspreads altered with the seasons. Furniture would come and go. The landlords who owned the house changed at least three to four times, each transition a source of anxiety to my parents, who always feared having to move. But the apartment remained a constant—a stable place where my brother and I were born and lived until we married. Though my family often looked at houses in Brooklyn and Staten Island and almost bought one down the block, my parents backed out, fearful that the payments would restrict everyday life. "The meat," my mother would say, shaking her head firmly. "We have to make sure we can afford the meat." It seemed right that my parents came with us when we closed on our Durham house. Its generational force marked the success of my parents' dreams.

My house—soon not to be my house—is a beauty. It has a gracious, mid-century modern flow, lots of light, and, what counts most I think, an abundance of happy memories. My older daughter was an adorable fourteen months when we moved in, all chubby wobbly legs and dark brown curls, cascading around the place with her favorite bottle of apple juice in hand. My younger daughter was born slightly more than a year later, during a Guggenheim fellowship year, when I also finished a book. Productive me went from being an assistant to a full professor in that house, from being a published but still uncertain author to achieving what felt like my own voice. Over time, whenever we had the cash, we lovingly furnished or renovated almost every inch. The house felt lucky and collected happy memories. It was celebratory, the food almost sacramental. Selling it was a confession, always *triste*, of how much life had changed. For if the house had symbolized arrival, personally and professionally, giving it up signaled a possible decline that felt premature. It was "downsizing"—a dreary metaphor that cloaks with a smiley face the shrinking of late middle and old age.

The night we told our daughters the house was going on the market, my younger daughter tried to be stoic but then broke down on the phone. She wouldn't be able to show the house to her own children, she said; she would never, ever see us all together in a place she had first seen with a toddler's eyes. No deck would ever seem so special; the wallpaper in the bathroom would never be so dazzling; the cardinals in the trees wouldn't seem, somehow, as red. The past would be lost, and no amount of searching would ever bring it back. All true. The past had been a thing of richness and plentitude, and I was not eager to shed it. I told her, and myself, that history and memories do not reside in any meaningful way in a house. They reside in people and in us. But was I lying? Or at least not yet telling the whole truth?

For of course, and perhaps inevitably, the very things that tie my daughter to the house became the reasons it was time to leave. The wallpaper in the bathroom my daughter so admires has been hanging for more than twenty years. Like the room itself, it could use an update and was even on the verge of getting shabby. The same could be said for the kitchen—bigger than any kitchen I'll ever have again but with old painted cabinets. Not to mention the large back deck we'd built, now rounding fifteen years. Those sprightly cardinals flitting in and around our very private acre-plus of land form, truly, one of the glories of the place. They're a sight that never stopped thrilling some part of me. But our land, like any land, needed trees removed, shrubs trimmed, lawns reseeded—not to mention regular maintenance. Some years, the expense could be dramatic. Once, Southern pine beetles ravaged forty trees, and removing them cost over four thousand dollars. I can still remember getting that news in Iowa, where I was visiting the University of Iowa, and not being sure at all how we'd pay on top of the sudden need, the same year, to replace an aging septic system we had not even known we had.

Let's face it, as we tried to do: Our house was glorious but maintenance intensive. Was it nice for two people? Yes. Would it make a great place to retire and take us into old age? Yes, once more. Was it necessary for two people? No. Was it sensible for people with our current lifestyle? No, and emphatically no again. For here again, life dealt me a twist, one it took me years to fully process.

By 2001, I had begun to teach away from campus for months each year, leading a program called Duke in New York—first for four months, then more than six. My large Durham house became a burden, with renters dicey and (as university folk) barely willing to cover our costs. Finding a new place to live in New York City each year becomes unthinkable for anyone who knows the crazy market, let alone for someone with a strong homing instinct, like me. After a few years, I began to rent an apartment in the city, eventually buying and furnishing first one very small apartment, then trading it in for two others over four years before settling down in a Greenwich Village "junior four" with a view.

The problem—not surprisingly—was that it no longer made sense to have a large and elegant home in Durham for only part of the year, especially a high-maintenance one where things went wrong each time we were away. And even if it did made sense, once we purchased a big-enough apartment in New York, we could no longer afford to do so.

So, where did that leave me? With the need, the real and practical need, to sell the house and "downsize."

Unreal Estate

"Unreal estate" refers to the memory of people who are gone, places that have vanished from our lives, the past itself. It's Vladimir Nabokov's supple phrase in his classic autobiography *Speak Memory* (1951), along with "intangible property"—some of it, in his case, reimagined from a distance of fifty years. Regardless of age, we all have unreal estate and intangible property becoming bigger parts of our portfolios all the time. There's no mortgage on unreal estate, no possible bubble, except for the delusions caused by the past. Only limited renovations are ever needed, or even possible—though, as with regular real estate, maintenance remains ongoing.

As *Crossing Back* draws to a close, the daily meditation practice it describes surfaced saturated moments out of time: vivid memories about the beloved dead. The memories advanced the goal of the book: to access shards of memory, without pain.

The memory of my father came to me in a flash, with the vivid tangibility of unreal estate. I was seven or eight at the time, and we were, as we were many weekends, at my cousin Nick's house in Islip, which was then a rural and little-known Long Island town on the southern shore, where we'd lower crab traps from the local piers. My Uncle Joe would drive us, slowly, as was his wont, in his sturdy black Ford that looked like something out of a 1930s movie, guided at each turn by my Aunt Minnie, his much-needed navigator. I resemble Minnie physically, though not as much as I resemble my mother. I can still see her round face and thin, curly hair, dyed red as she grew older; her cheerful yet also somehow dour face behind clear-framed glasses; and her slightly pinched mouth, which could say things that were wry and funny or bad tempered.

Nick's house was fairly simple—a bungalow really, with a yard. There was a rose garden where I loved the bushes. At night, we'd light a fire in a trash can—an odd hobo's habit in a stable family. We'd play cards or sing the kind of nonsensical and often somewhat vulgar songs that are part of Italian-American tradition, which abounds in puns and innuendos. If you've seen the wedding scene in Coppola's *The Godfather* or heard a CD called *Mob Hits*, you know the kind of thing I mean: "Get outta here with your boom-boom-boom [just a sound here, accompanied by a rude arm gesture] and don't come back no more!" What was a "boom-boom-boom?" I'd wonder.

The back of the house faced an open field that was used to train race horses, with a circular track and then a heavily treed road paved in gravel that led to a highway. One Sunday, my father and I sat for a lazy afternoon making kites out of the newspaper comics. I remember picking and choosing which pages would show on my kite and which would be glued and hidden. My father chose his own, with a flourish. I remember feeling like it was a miracle to see kites take shape out of some sticks, newspaper, tape, and glue. Late that day, toward sunset, the glue was dry, the wind picked up, and the kites took flight. We ran along the yard and along the track, and the kites looked wonderful against the deep blue summer sky. Then, for reasons I don't recall—maybe bravado, maybe just a desire for a change of scene—we started up the gravel road that led to the paved road. We ran here too and the kites kept pace, flying up high against the darkening blue. Until, as we were about to enter the main road, my kite caught on a telephone wire near a tree.

I can still see my father running down the road—tall, lanky, his tongue protruding between his teeth, as often happened when he was concentrating. I can feel the fresh air, the waning sunshine, and the slight cooling of the coming evening sky. I can recall the effort Dad put into retrieving that kite— shimmying up the tree and using various sticks and branches. But it was just out of reach and would not budge. He offered me his kite, but, as any child will know, that wouldn't and couldn't be the same. We walked back down the road, his arm around my shoulders. And he said, in the boisterous voice I always considered, somehow, faux boisterous: "Well, but we had fun, anyway, didn't we?" I don't know whether I agreed at the time. But I sure do now. We had fun. I wonder, if he were selecting a memory, a bit of unreal estate, what he'd choose.

The memory of my mother is more vexed and awkward. It's not filled, or not at first glance, with the joy of the outdoors or of flying a kite. I find it odd but telling that I recalled it most of all. Unlike the memory of my father, it's tied not to a house but to a vividly remembered classroom.

Unlike many of the mothers in my elementary school class, my mother worked and so was not available for field trips or parties. One day, the class was scheduled to listen to a radio broadcast, from the United Nations I think. It may have been to commemorate its founding, but the subject is not important or germane. Listening to the radio in class was still a big thing back then, so the teacher announced that there would be refreshments and that we should invite our mothers—fathers, it was understood, would be working.

As a garment worker, a finisher who checked buttons and snipped threads, my mother experienced seasonal layoffs when she'd routinely collect unemployment insurance and nominally (though not really) look for another job until things "picked up." It was one of those seasons; she was waiting for things to "pick up." I invited her to class and, when she said she'd come, invested some time and energy imagining what it would be like. She arrived on time, dressed in a suit, with a white blouse, gloves, and simple pumps. Her hair was short and curled and nice. She looked like a lady.

When the radio went on, I recall her holding her purse in her lap and straining to look attentive and interested in the broadcast. Whatever it was— I've blanked it out—was so dull I felt mortified. The refreshments were meager, and, what's worse, no one else's mother came, so that I could tell Mom felt uncomfortable.

I find it such an unpleasant bit of unreal estate, until a friend points out that I'm thinking from the point of view of an embarrassed child feeling bad about having put her mother in an awkward spot. In a different key, the scene reads as an act of love, different from my father with the kite, but typical of my mother, who showed her love indirectly. For if I invested effort in that day, as I did, my mother had too. She wore white gloves and was careful to look nice. She was showing love through things, as she often did—good food, new clothes—like the time she'd splurged, and I knew it, to buy me an extra dress at A&S in downtown Brooklyn, an A-line, short-sleeved number in Kelly green that I still remember vividly. The memories of my mother in her suit and of that Kelly-green dress remain part of my unreal estate.

Moving House

The story of selling my Durham house to this point has been particular to my family—even, perhaps, to me. The actual process of selling the house was more generic and, as usual, exciting and boring all at once—so I'll move quickly. In March, when the house went on the market, we learned how to be prepared, at any moment, for a "showing": house clean, desks clear, flowers out, candles lit, and all the rest. In *The God of Small Things*, Arundhati Roy notes that *paravans* (untouchables) in the old days were required to sweep away all evidence of their footsteps in the dust as they walked. Getting ready for a "showing" is like that. It's the art of making yourself disappear in the place where you live, making it as close as possible to a neutral, model house. For Italians, always aware of *la bella figura* (looking good to others), the process is, perhaps, a bit easier than for most. But let's face it, being "shown" on short notice is uncomfortable and unsettling. It's a bit like living in a whorehouse.

As the weeks passed without a sale, we set a deadline. In Italian-American terms, I made what I call a fate-bet: If the house had not sold by the time we returned to Durham from New York, we would take it off the market and rent it during an upcoming sabbatical. On the last possible day before the deadline, a far-too-low offer on our house turned plausible, and, within a week, the house was sold. Perhaps oddly, though it did not seem odd to me, I felt happy that the buyer loved the house and did not plan to tear it down to build a McMansion. He liked knowing that, since 1963, only two families had owned the house. I liked knowing that I had remained loyal to the house, even in selling it.

More than a decade later, I still drive by my old house from time to time—well, actually almost every time I am in Southwest Durham—noting the changes made by the new owner. I liked some of them, as when he painted its practical pinkish-brick a stylish light gray that matched the roof: a killer change that stressed the house's horizontal lines. A well-heeled businessman, he not only built a pond in the wooded far yard for his dogs but gated the driveway, which seemed pretentious. I still hear from this man from time to time, and he invites me to visit, though I always decline. Seeing the inside again would feel like finding Ellie, my beloved stuffed elephant, in the sordid trash cans of New York.

After the sale, we looked for a new house, setting a deadline here as well, since I was lucky enough to be teaching in Venice beginning in late May. We found the new house precisely on the deadline: small enough to be easier to maintain, inexpensive enough to make sense, in a heavily wooded neighborhood close to the university, with trees, greenery, and red cardinals in the yard. In fact, the house was a pint-size version of the original full quart, but not so similar that it felt like moving just next door.

By moving day, utter exhaustion ran interference with so many other emotions that it checked any impulse to feel sad, even though, when I began this recollection, the tears came quick and plenty. I'd always thought that our things made our house so lovely. Now, cleared and cleaned, the house revealed its secret, the secret that my father knew the day we moved in. Its high ceilings and well-proportioned rooms glow in light; the wood floors we installed show off good bones. Emptied of our things, the house resembled a stage set after a play has ended. Clean, symmetrical, and organized around its cathedral ceilings, as a classical stage might be around its pillars or a ghost light. The action, or my part in it at least, had ended. Like the stage, the house would come to life, with others. But now it was bare and about to be stripped of me.

Unreal Estate by Proxy

My meditations turned up no single memory of my brother; instead, it surfaced two. One is the memory of a photo—unreal estate piled on unreal estate. He's about one or one and a half in the photo, and so, if I existed yet (as I rather suspect I did not), I would have been a newborn baby. He has lustrous, long, dark curls and was destined within the next few months to have his first haircut and be shorn and masculine.

My brother's face is puckered, and he's crying his heart out, as though the world just wasn't acting right or was not quite good enough. I can imagine the cajoling and distractions he was offered. A bottle. A biscuit. A toy. But he wouldn't stop, and the photographer my parents visited that day just could not get a smiling picture. And so my brother's most typical baby portrait shows him crying.

The second memory connects by theme to masculinity. When we were very young—three and five, four and six perhaps, but no older than that, I should think—we were being bathed together by my mother. Our hair had been washed with Johnson's baby shampoo; our flesh had been scrubbed clean of the day's play. There must have been some kind of dispute about who got to do something first, with my mother deciding, as she often would, that my brother would get his way because "he's the boy." Toweling down, I said with some derision: "What's so special about having a little mushroom down there?" It was what Freud would consider classic penis envy, except that I meant it literally, with no envy at all. It was also a non sequitur. Our childhood baths stopped that day, though we shared a room in the small apartment for at least another five to seven years.

In my meditations, a memory of my own childhood became a proxy memory that my infant son Matthew never got to have, or, at least, to express. The memory resonates with Virginia Woolf's *The Waves*, a novel I have written about, in which each character has a shattering moment in early childhood, discovering that a boundary exists between the self and the outside world.

I was young, perhaps three or four, and once again in the yard at my cousin's house in Islip. It was early morning or just getting dark—one or the other. I remember only that the light was striking and unusual. I've always loved to make up stories, and I was singing and talking to a rose bush. I suspect that I was telling this bush some favorite story, not yet making the kind of distinctions an older child would between people and things, inside and outside. My Aunt Minnie came looking for me and, seeing and hearing what I was up to, called out loudly, "Hey. Rose. She's out here and the kid is talking to a rose bush!" She might have thought it was cute; she might have thought it was weird—my Aunt Minnie could have gone either way. But the effect for me was like the scene in *Bananas* when Woody Allen's character purchases porn magazines, adding numerous other items he can't afford to make the purchase less noticeable, and the store clerk calls out, in a loud voice so that everyone in the store can hear, "Hey Ralph, how much is a copy of *Orgasm?*" Even as a child, I felt mortified.

Matthew taught me a lot—not all of it happy by any means. But I remember discovering by observing him, far more effectively than by reading Lacan, why so many people marry those who resemble them, often in the configuration of eyes and nose.

My son was two, maybe three months old, not far away from his premature ending, and dressed in an adorable outfit in Kelly green. (Kelly green: Family history and unreal estate work through uncanny repetitions; so does reality.) He was on a dressing table where it was secure to leave him for a few minutes. When I turned back, he was touching his face in the mirror and smiling, cooing, clearly having fallen in love with his own image. "Who's that?" he would have said, had there been words. "You're pretty great and I love you!" He didn't process the image as himself at all—any more than a cat does when you hold it up to a mirror. He was floating—as was I with the rose bush—in moments that come often for children and still happen from time to time throughout life, when we feel at one with the universe and in love with everything around us, including that good-looking person in the mirror there. Real estate. Unreal estate.

Coda

"Welcome home!" my meditation teacher says when I've been gone, traveling or in North Carolina—and to all of us when we come out of meditation. Is he, as he says, a little strange, having meditated for more than fifty years? Is he just being warm and nice? Or does he sense something that he's acknowledged from time to time in compliments about the steadiness of my breath and smooth facial expression? He called me "quiet" once in a private session I booked to ask permission to quote him in this book, which he freely gave. Quiet: which I'm not. Until I realized that I really am quiet in his studio, rarely needing and never demanding his attention before or after class, as many people do.

In recent years, meditation has become a vogue and a fad, nurtured, among other things, by the success of Elizabeth Gilbert's *Eat, Pray, Love*. The worst scenes in the movie version show Julia Roberts sitting with her legs crossed and her hands in *gian mudra* (palms up, thumb touching the index finger)—a pose we are supposed to read as "acquiring tranquility and wisdom." The shots are annoying. Except that people really do acquire more tranquility and wisdom in meditation, if they stick with it—or, at least, more tranquility. Meditation has been practiced for centuries, in the East and West—extended

prayer and chanting being forms of meditation, too. Science has caught up to
what yogis have known for centuries: Meditation slows the breath and calms
the mind and even, over time, changes it. Most of all, meditation gives a different feeling for what is, and is not, important.

Al's brand of yoga is tantric, a term that does not mean merely "sexual"—a
common misunderstanding in America—but *worldly*. It's yoga that expects
the practitioner to live an ordinary, everyday life. Though esoteric Tantrism in
India can be highly sexed, tantric yogis in the United States are householders,
like you and me. They don't isolate themselves in ashrams, they don't espouse
vows of chastity to heighten spirituality, nor do they cultivate edgy sex. Basically, they seek balance rather than extremes, adopting practices and traditions
as they please without feeling the need for a single, pure method.

"If it works, use it!" Al says cheerfully to most of the questions people ask
him about meditation. He doesn't care how many beats we hold our breath
or how precisely we hold our fingers. He doesn't care whether we do perfect
down dogs or planks. "It doesn't matter," he told me in that private session.
"We're all going to die anyway." Working quickly, Al tries and mostly succeeds
in generating a feeling of transcendence, in Manhattan, in sixty minutes. It is
a compromise, he knows—what he calls a taste of samadhi.

"You know those puppies people put in cars, the ones with loose, floaty
heads?" Al says. He bounces his own, generous-sized head from side to side to
show what he means. Immediately, the black-and-white little dogs he means,
the equivalent of a hula dancer on a dashboard, leap to mind. "That's good,
when the head is loose and floating. The way the Indians do and we can't."
And he gives another shake. This teacher's constant good humor proves infec-
tious—it's his "job," he says, and it gives him now, into his seventies, a childlike
air. His appearance may not be a model of physical perfection, resembling, as
he frequently says while pointing to a statue, "this fellow here," Ganesh, the
elephant. Al has paunchy abs, what he calls a "deluxe body," and not a yoga
teacher's more typical six-pack. Still, when Alan demonstrates a forward bend
or a leg lift or simply a deep breath, it's clear to anyone who sees him that he
has power—a natural gift via his yogi father, honed by decades of practice.

"You should know where you are going after death," Al says sometimes at
meditation, laughing jovially. "We can love life and should! Enjoy it! It's good!
But we can't stop time. We're all going to die. *Maha-samadhi*, the big game,
Super Bowl Sunday!" It's a joke, comparing the moment of death to America's
football feast day—a joke of the kind Al almost always makes when he introduces death. It's his way of reaching the twenty-somethings who flock to his
meditations, without scaring them off. But he's utterly serious about death as
the ultimate state of samadhi.

The Tibetan *Book of the Dead* says that a good death recognizes and follows energy pathways out of the body. Meditation helps prepare you for that. In meditation, you clear a space in your mind and surrender to find those pathways as a preparation not just for life but also for death. You make your mind an empty space, stripped and bare, but still well lit and recognizably lovely.

"Rental!" Al says, again jokingly, though he is telling the simple truth; "our bodies are rental—water and chemicals and a bag of bones—but they're our vehicle for going through this life." Yoga and meditation do not deny bodily pleasures, which are considerable. But they do teach, over time, that the absence of you, in the body, is the final meaning of selling the house. You survive in memories and in the ghost light of your energy. But the stage is stripped, the screen ready for the next movie.

As I write, I'm in my cozy forest house in Durham, North Carolina, where I rarely spent more than two months at a time until the COVID-19 pandemic. Al's yoga home, my yoga home, too, is empty for now, existing only online. Al himself has relocated to Florida, to be near family. Yet, like music, gardening, or drama sessions for others, yoga and meditation have formed a community for me, one that does not (I've learned) require a roof or walls. What links us is, ultimately, the stillness and the unity always available in meditation.

When you come out of meditation, slowly regrounding the body, and go back to everyday things—the going back being absolutely essential—your body feels relaxed, your mind clear, your back unknotted, fluid, and "green at the spine." Welcome home.

The Stark but Familiar Allure
of Empty Cities

An Epilogue

In January 2020, three months before America locked down, I remember seeing images of how China was handling COVID-19 and saying to my husband, "Can you believe Shanghai could be so empty? Can you imagine trying that in New York?" At the time, we could not. Soon, New York became the epicenter of the pandemic, and, like many others, we retreated from the city to our house in North Carolina. We continued to feel concerned about the city and asked about it often, following the news. We also felt fascinated by photographs of New York's empty streets that, along with others from 2020, seemed stark but also strangely familiar.

Shanghai deserted, where many thousands would throng. Sparse train stations in Mumbai. The lovely but empty squares of Paris with, perhaps, a solitary walker to mark the scale. Even cities that usually have far too many tourists looked suddenly bereft. St Mark's Square in Venice, with the usual pigeons, but no people. The Rialto Bridge, empty and shuttered. New York, Chicago, San Francisco, Los Angeles. The empty cities of 2020 were not dead; their inhabitants had withdrawn, for a time, to save lives—their own and others. But they struck the mind as simulacra of places where civilization has ended completely or human life has vanished, for good.

The images evoked things we had seen before in fiction but never so dramatically and in real time. Films, TV shows, video games, and novels show empty cities quite often, especially as part of nuclear war or virus plots. Older movies like 1959's *On the Beach* and *The World, the Flesh, and the Devil* posit that radiation has made humans vanish, with not a corpse in sight, but with buildings and infrastructure totally intact—as if after some crazy worldwide Rapture.[1] Newer ones like *I Am Legend* portray a world devastated by a vaccine gone wrong—creepy to think about in 2020 and 2021. New York's Central Park, a cornfield, tumbleweeds on Fifth Avenue, urban pastoral without shepherds.[2]

Novels like Emily St. John Mandel's *Station Eleven* and Lawrence Wright's *The End of October* play out in detail the aftereffects of devastating pandemics.[3] I read both books early during quarantine, more aware than ever of the blessings of electricity and a functioning social world. Even nonfiction like Alan Weisman's *The World without Us* and the History Channel's *Life after People*, which resolutely refuse to speculate on why humans have vanished, display image after image, metric after metric of how nature or animals would reclaim empty cities.[4] Video games like *Tokyo Jungle* show animals taking over the town.[5] Life echoing the imagination, during 2020 many people, including me, noticed exuberant bird, vegetable, and plant life, even on familiar walks. People posted zucchini and tomato porn from their gardens. Videos of wild animals in major cities went viral—bunnies, foxes, deer, and coyotes—how amazing to see them in urban neighborhoods!

What drives our fascination with empty cities, a virtual contradiction in terms? In part, they remind us how fragile our great cities and their cultures become after disasters. They whisper that, someday, we'll be gone, with our buildings remaining behind, if they remain at all, as giant, glistering tombstones. Empty cities warn us that the incredible systems humans create won't be permanent, especially if we do not learn to respect our limitations and nature's power. Like Angor Wat in Cambodia, Petra in Jordan, and Knossos on Crete, lost cities from the past that I have visited whisper that same message and reveal even more about the oddly intoxicating allure of empty cities.

The summer before my mother died, I was lucky enough to teach for the first time in Venice, living for two months above a charming flower shop that put out its wares every morning in a small *campiello*, a miniature Venetian square. I loved waking up with my morning coffee, opening the window, and surveying the scene. It now strikes me as odd, even extremely odd, that I did not give a second thought to leaving my ninety-year-old mother in New York while I taught and then traveled in Europe for ten full weeks. When I came home, she didn't seem quite like herself, saying that she'd serve just one course on Sundays rather than the usual two or three. When I said that would be fine, but asked why, my mother said she felt tired. My mother, Rose, who had always been so strong, too tired to cook. Four months later, my mother died, sending me spinning.

None of that was on my mind as I entered Pompeii that summer, a living city near Naples whose fame depends on a dead one. I'd brought my class to see its ruins, now a theme park devoted to the 79 CE eruption of Mount

Vesuvius. On our visit, we passed pubs and pub signs. Brothels and the amusingly vulgar lingams that mark them. Tilework and wall murals in sexy red and black depicting dancing, dining, and festive bacchanalia. And then, and a highlight of the tour, corpses old and young mummified by lava and ash in positions of flight. My students loved it.

Yet the name "Pompeii" instantly evokes lives snuffed out within minutes, amid fleshly enjoyments. A momento mori, it tells a cautionary tale about the awesome power of nature: Sodom and Gomorrah, ripe for natural destruction. Just as these ancient citizens lost everything, all at once, the tale goes, so might you. Before nature, we humans remain puny and, sometimes, powerless.

In the American Southwest, at sites like Mesa Verde and Canyon de Chelly, stone structures like giant dollhouses slice into mountains and survive, although the civilizations that built them did not. Petroglyphs depict animals and hunts, and they remain partly legible mysteries. There were hunts; there were hunters: That much is clear. But who were the people in the images? And why did they leave the places we can see today, which seem protected from conquest? Was there a drought, a virus, or a pathogen like those documented for certain Mayan sites?[6] A possibility newly chilling after the COVID-19 pandemic. We will, perhaps, never truly know, and that's part of lost cities' powerful allure: They harbor stories just waiting to be told, yet tantalizingly out of reach. Mystery, on our pulses. They suggest the Burkean sublime: great beauty, with an undertow of danger. They remind us that we humans are small and probably temporary things on Earth.

A famous, bustling port when St. Paul wrote his Epistles and St. John referenced it in the Book of Revelation, Ephesus in Turkey now sits about fifty miles inland. Centuries of silt deposited by the Kaystros River have cut it off from the Aegean Sea, once the core of its identity. The city was also partially destroyed by an earthquake in 614 CE. Five minutes into a visit, it's possible to feel disappointed. After a long trip and a tedious bus transfer, the structures in Ephesus are very nice but, or so it seems, just a block of well-preserved Roman houses. Then, turning a corner, a surprise and a gasp.

Long avenues unfold, with many excavated and well-preserved buildings leading to a gigantic library with grand, impressive steps. Scrambling up the rows of a large amphitheater, it's easy to imagine public forums, plays, or, perhaps, the grimmer fare of gladiators or martyrs. Ephesus embodies the history of both imperial Rome and of early Christianity. It allows visitors tactile access to a sensuous, vivid past—and that's part of its allure.

But perhaps the most arresting fact today about a city like Ephesus is how it died because of climate change. Once powerful and a crossroads of civilizations, its citizens deserted Ephesus after geography left it vulnerable to gradual but inexorable natural forces. Water and sand, erasing commerce and culture. As climate change becomes climate catastrophe, Ephesus issues a prophetic warning to today's great cities. Ephesus then; Venice soon; New York, New Orleans, Miami, San Francisco, Mumbai, Shanghai soon enough.

The chill of natural disaster, whether eruption, drought, disease, or flood; sudden death; mystery and the Burkean sublime; history and spirit: Only the faint of heart and imagination don't feel the thrill of history's lost cities. When we behold empty cities from the past, when we beheld the empty cities of 2020, we feel anew both the fascination and the fear of events that might be coming soon to neighborhoods near us.

At the end of the last chapter, I say that "the absence of you, in the body, is the final meaning of selling the house" and that savasana, the corpse pose that ends yoga classes, imitates death. I believe both statements to be true. The fate that empty cities portend—loss of populations, even the end of civilization—might sit relatively easily with someone like me, a practicing yogi who meditates daily, placing time-present in an eternal framework. For at least thirty years, mindfulness meditation has taught people to see their thoughts but to remain detached; for much longer, religions have taught the transience of human life. The yoga traditions I follow cultivate "the witnessing mind," which is able to maintain a sense of equanimity and balance amid temporal flux by accessing a far larger, cosmic perspective. The lessons that empty cities teach should be ones I am willing to hear. The world we cling to is like a movie that unrolls before our eyes and then vanishes. Maya. It's all maya, illusion, with some greater power or cosmic energy that is not impressed by humans and what they have made.

Far less than "not impressed." Neutral and even indifferent. God or, if we will, the force that moves the universe is not hostile to humanity. We've had our chance and still do if we could commit to undoing centuries of damage, as we probably won't. But, like time itself in Virginia Woolf's *To the Lighthouse*, nature ultimately does not care that much about our fate. We make it. Or we don't. Either way, one way or another, life will persist. The energy of the universe still throbs.

I hear that message in a surprising number of the "what if" stories being told today in popular novels, like Richard Powers's majestic *The Overstory*. A host of recent popular science books suggest that too: *How Forests Think: Towards an Anthropology beyond Human*; *The Hidden Life of Trees: What They Feel, How They Communicate*; *Underland: A Deep Time Journey*.[7] These books imagine a future in which Earth's sentient beings (a sovereign "They") include trees, but not humans. Science-based projections say much the same:

Roy Scranton's *Learning to Die in the Anthropocene* (2015); David Wallace-Wells's "The Uninhabitable Earth" (2019); Bill McKibben's "130 Degrees." Indeed, as McKibben says, the COVID-19 crisis may be the first of many worldwide emergencies as climate change becomes climate catastrophe.[8]

Like the pandemic of 2020–2021, like 2020 as a whole, such facts feel overwhelming at times. Being only human, no more than that, I hear them sadly and with regret. Thinking about the future, I knock on wood.

Notes

Prologue

1. Statistics in this Prologue are as of Sunday, May 9, 2021.

2. Edwidge Danticat, "Mourning in Place," *New York Review of Books* 67, no. 14 (September 24, 2020), https://www.nybooks.com/articles/2020/09/24/mourning-in-place/.

3. "An Incalculable Loss," *New York Times*, May 27, 2020, https://www.nytimes.com/interactive/2020/05/24/us/us-coronavirus-deaths-100000.html.

4. Among the first accounts of losses at Hiroshima is John Hersey, *Hiroshima* (New York: Knopf, 1946), which originally appeared as a special edition of the *New Yorker*. It remained one of the few sources for a very long time. See my *The War Complex: World War II in Our Time* (Chicago: University of Chicago Press, 2003), 6–7, 100–1; and Lesley M. M. Blum, *Fallout: The Hiroshima Cover-Up and the Reporter Who Revealed It* (New York: Simon and Schuster, 2020). On 9/11, see the *New York Times'* "Portraits of Grief" series. In the vast literature of the Holocaust that followed Raul Hilberg's and Saul Friedlander's landmark work, personal testimony by Primo Levi and the literature of Elie Wiesel stand out; the Binjamin Wilkomirski scandal of 1991 showed a strong recoil about false witness testimony.

5. Georges Bataille, "Concerning the Accounts Given by the Residents of Hiroshima" (1947), rpt. in Cathy Caruth, *Trauma: Explorations in Memory* (Baltimore, MD: Johns Hopkins University Press, 1991).

6. A chart published by the Center for Disease Control (CDC) makes the case very clearly: https://www.cdc.gov/coronavirus/2019-ncov/covid-data/investigations-discovery/hospitalization-death-by-race-ethnicity.html. The percentages of those able to work from home or not were based on CDC figures as well: https://www.cdc.gov/coronavirus/2019-ncov/community/health-equity/race-ethnicity.html.

7. *PBS Newshour*, December 17, 2020.

8. Military records list 291,557 combat deaths in World War II. Combat deaths in World War I are commonly listed as 53,402; in Vietnam, 47,434. See https://www.va.gov/opa/publications/factsheets/fs_americas_wars.pdf.

9. The literature on individual and cultural memory is large. Classic sources include Maurice Halbachs, *On Collective Memory*, ed. and trans. Lewis A. Coser (Chicago: University of Chicago Press, 1993), a compendium of Halbachs's writing on the topic. Walter Benjamin makes some interesting observations about shock and its relationship to memory in *Illuminations*, ed. Hannah Arendt (New York: Schocken, 1969), observations that might lead to the huge literature on trauma and trauma theory. Other theorists worth noting include Jacques Rancière and Jürgen Habermas. I discuss the topic in my *The War Complex*, 3–11.

10. Matt Stevens, Isabella Grullón Paz, and Jennifer Medina, "Kristin Urquiza, Whose Father Died of Covid, Denounces Trump at DNC," *New York Times*, August 17, 2020, https://www.nytimes.com/2020/08/17/us/politics/kristin-urquiza-dad-covid-trump.html.

11. "He Warned of Coronavirus. Here's What He Told Us before He Died," *New York Times*, February 7, 2020, https://www.nytimes.com/2020/02/07/world/asia/Li-Wenliang-china-coronavirus.html.

12. Jesmyn Ward, "On Witness and Respair: A Personal Tragedy Followed by Pandemic," *Vanity Fair*, September 1, 2020, https://www.vanityfair.com/culture/2020/08/jesmyn-ward-on-husbands-death-and-grief-during-covid.

13. Louise DeSalvo, *Crazy in the Kitchen: Food, Feuds, and Forgiveness in an Italian American Family* (New York: Bloomsbury, 2005), 241.

14. Bill McKibben makes the case starkly that COVID-19 gave us a foretaste of global crises that are likely to become more and more intractable as the twenty-first century unrolls. "130 Degrees," *New York Review of Books* 67, no. 13 (August 20, 2020).

Introduction

1. Marianna Torgovnick, *Crossing Ocean Parkway* (Chicago: University of Chicago Press, 1993), 10. Hereafter cited parenthetically as COP.

2. Roland Barthes, *Mourning Diary: October 26, 1977–September 15, 1979* (New York: Hill and Wang, 2016), 38.

3. Renato Rosaldo, "Grief and a Headhunter's Rage," in *Culture and Truth: Remaking the Social Analysis* (New York: Routledge, 1989), 395.

4. Susan Sontag, *Regarding the Pain of Others* (New York: Picador, 2004).

5. Christopher Beha, *The Whole Five Feet: What the Great Books Taught Me about Life, Death, and Pretty Much Everything Else* (New York: Grove, 2009); Nina Sankovitch, *Tolstoy and the Purple Chair: My Year of Magical Reading* (New York: Harper Collins, 2011); Joseph Luzzi, *In a Dark Wood: What Dante Taught Me about Grief, Healing, and the Mysteries of Love* (New York: Harper Wave, 2015); Helen MacDonald, *H Is for Hawk* (New York: Harper, 2016).

6. A 2010 bestseller by Hubert Dreyfus and Sean Dorrance Kelly called *All Things*

Shining: Reading the Western Classics to Find Meaning in a Secular Age (New York: Free Press, 2010) contrasts the mindset of the ancient Greeks with modernity in a way I found derivative of Georg Lukács but riddled by misreadings of important texts. It was not the only book I consulted about reading the classics; see, among others, David Denby, *Great Books: My Adventures with Homer, Rousseau, Woolf, and Other Indestructible Writers of the Western World* (New York: Simon & Schuster, 1996); and Jay Parini, *Promised Land: Thirteen Books That Changed America* (New York: Doubleday, 2008).

7. Benjamin's essay "The Work of Art in the Age of Mechanical Reproduction," originally published in 1935, appeared in English in 1968, in a collection Hannah Arendt edited called *Illuminations*. Jay Parini represents how Benjamin gave the manuscript to Arendt in a novel called *Benjamin's Crossing* (New York: Holt, 1996).

8. A tip of the hat to James Mirollo, a teacher at Columbia University who used to say, "You've got to read Aristotle." In this case, the *Poetics* and the theory of catharsis.

9. Malouf reimagines the fabulous scene when Priam travels to Achilles's tent to request the dead body of his son, Hector, highlighting both men as fathers and sons. Miller uses some arcane sources to expand the usual myths of Circe.

10. See Marianna Torgovnick, *Primitive Passions: Men, Women, and the Quest for Ecstasy* (New York: Knopf, 1997).

1. Living Tissue

1. Not a subject for bragging rights at all, my parents and brother died of cancer or complications from treatment, as did several uncles on both sides of my family and four to five first cousins.

2. Siddhartha Mukherjee, *The Emperor of Maladies: A Biography of Cancer* (New York: Scribner's, 2010), 462, 6, 388. Mukherjee adds that, in the human genome, cancer cells' language is "grammatical, methodical, and even—I hesitate to write— quite beautiful" (454). The last phrase goes all the way to where Sigmund Freud went hesitantly in 1922, in *Civilization and Its Discontents*, in a rare passage where he takes the oceanic sensation seriously instead of seeing it as a pathology. See my *Primitive Passions* (New York: Knopf, 1997), 11–12, 15.

3. That, in part, is why new targeted gene therapies, as opposed to chemotherapy, seem so promising.

4. The coined word recurs in David Malouf, *Ransom: A Novel* (New York: Pantheon, 2009).

5. I am indebted for the phrase I use as this section's title to Malouf's *Ransom*.

6. The printed version of the play references Sophocles's *Electra* and (less frequently) Euripides's *Iphigenia at Aulis*, as well as its basic source, the *Oresteia*, especially its second play, *The Libation Bearers*. The program notes add a reference to Sartre's *The Flies* as well, where Electra is less significant than Orestes. I used the Penguin Classics edition of Aeschylus's *The Oresteia*, trans. Robert Fagles (1979).

7. The summary contains several elements that are anachronistic within the setting of the plays: Human sacrifice was already a relic, and the legend of Odysseus and Penelope has an aura of matriarchy hinted at in the role Clytemnestra assumes but rejects.

8. See *In Search of Troy*, dir. and narr. Michael Wood (BBC2, 1985); updated book version (Berkeley: University of California Press, 1998). The *Odyssey* describes figures it dislikes, like Achilles, as leading their men "in plunder," not battle.

9. Atreus's primal crime and Aegisthus's link to the same lineage loom large in Aeschylus's trilogy—less so in *Molora*.

10. While years pass between *Agamemnon* and *The Libation Bearers*, the indication is for "several," but not seventeen, years. Homer's *Odyssey* specifies eight years in its telling of the story, which accuses Aegisthus of Agamemnon's murder and praises Orestes.

11. *Molora* changes Aeschylus's plot from this point on.

12. I do not know the origins of the phrase, Cancer World, which seems remarkably evocative. I saw it used in reviews of *The Emperor of All Maladies* but did not note it in the book itself. Steven Shapin wrote an article called "Cancer World: The Making of a Modern Disease," *New Yorker*, November 8, 2010, but I suspect the term originated earlier than that.

13. Investigation after my brother's death revealed that genetic links are relatively weak and route through the gene for early-onset breast cancer—not found in my family history. Testing for pancreatic cancer, moreover, is both unreliable and fairly useless; alertness to any sudden onset of diabetes, on the other hand, is not.

14. See "Slasher Stories," in my *Crossing Ocean Parkway* (Chicago: University of Chicago Press, 1993), 43–44.

15. My account of my father's illness became the final essay in *Crossing Ocean Parkway*.

16. "Adaptor-Director's Note," program for *Malora*, performed March 20, 2010, Reynolds Theater, Duke University.

17. The name of the mother given in the program is Cynthia Ngwenyu.

18. Archbishop Desmond Tutu chaired the commission and stressed *ubuntu*. Sophie Nield, "The Power of Speech," prefatory material to *Molora*. I would note the striking resemblance to the view of Zulu in Martin Buber's *I and Thou*, trans. Walter Kaufmann (1923; New York: Scribner's, 1970), 16; and to M. M. Bakhtin's recurring idea of the "dialogic imagination."

19. I was able to *identify* the language and the precise ethnicity of the actors only because of the program notes and a print edition of *Molora*. But the power of the performance did not depend on translation, and, in fact, I did not read the notes until afterward. The interplay between song, dance, language, and gestures remains both primary and entirely clear.

20. In the *Oresteia*, Orestes has fewer doubts, and no one urges him to heed them. He kills his mother and is then pursued by the Furies, who lose the right to kill him in a formal court. The jury's vote is, however, tied—so that, while sparing Orestes, the gods award the Furies dominion over the Underworld.

21. I learned later that the last three are the only professional actors in the group—a brilliant touch.

22. The fact comes from Hubert Dreyfus and Sean Dorrance Kelly, *All Things Shining: Reading the Western Classics to Find Meaning in a Secular Age* (New York: Free Press, 2010), 98; it gives no documentation.

23. A similar retelling and instance of what I call "living tissue" is Charles Mee's 2007 play *Iphigenia 2.0*.

2. Imagining Disaster

1. After a leisurely part 1, Woolf's part 2 encapsulates ten years in a very short section in which three characters—Mrs. Ramsay, her daughter Prue, and her son Andrew—die during World War I, with their passing recorded in parentheses. After its leisurely part 1, McEwan's novel suspends the action of part 2 with the hero, Robbie, wounded at Dunkirk. The novel then seems to grant him and his lover, Cecilia, a further and happy life. But we learn at the end that the narrator Briony's earlier betrayal can't be redeemed and that, despite her pretty fiction, both Robbie and Cecilia die early in the war.

2. *Austerlitz* as a whole requires the indirect imagination of violence. The section I have in mind here is the visit to Terezin and the still images frozen from a Nazi propaganda video.

3. Mother's Day

1. See Satchidananda's version of the *Sutras*: https://www.yogavedainstitute.com/wp-content/uploads/2018/06/Swami-Satchidananda-Yoga-Sutras-of-Patanjali.pdf.

2. In a sense, Pantanjali is like Homer, the man who wrote down a stable version of stories called the *Iliad* and the *Odyssey*.

3. See some important quotations from Iyengar, a powerful guru figure: https://www.doyouyoga.com/12-inspiring-quotes-from-b-k-s-iyengar-guru/.

4. Second Chances

1. Alice Kaplan encountered a similar smoker, described in *French Lessons: A Memoir* (Chicago: University of Chicago Press, 1993), for which I was an early reader.

2. Italo Calvino, "Why Read the Classics?" *New York Review of Books*, October 9, 1986, http://www.nybooks.com/articles/1986/10/09/why-read-the-classics/.

3. Though the relationship of fathers and sons is usually stressed in Greek epics, Nausicaa is very much a daughter in book 6 of the *Odyssey*.

4. Daniel Mendelsohn, *Odyssey: A Father, a Son, and an Epic* (New York: Knopf, 2017).

5. Though I compared translations, I use here Robert Fagles's colloquial prose version (1996; New York: Penguin, 2006).

6. Margaret Atwood compensates by giving the maids a more active role in her text. *The Penelopiad* (Edinburgh: Canongate, 2005), xv.

7. Mihoko Suzuki notes that "with Athena as its presiding deity, the *Odyssey* has been associated with the feminine before the rise of feminist criticism" in, for example, retellings by Samuel Butler and Robert Graves that use Nausicaa as a narrator. See Mihoko Suzuki, "Rewriting the *Odyssey* in the 21st Century," in *Approaches to Homer* (New York: Peter Lang, 2010), 239.

8. I use Samuel Butler's version of the line, which has become standard.

9. It's very odd, but I have no recollection of my grandfather's funeral and burial yet was clearly old enough to have been expected to be there.

10. My parents' relationship with my father's beloved nephew Nick and his family also ruptured around a ring. Repeating the repetitions so characteristic of family history and of myth, recent conflicts around a ring owned by my brother and claimed by both his widow and my nephew have ruptured their relationship.

11. Once again, with the repetitions characteristic of narrative, when I found a few photos of my mother in her bedroom, those were also discarded by the funeral home when my brother forgot to pick them up.

12. All quotations from *War and Peace* come from the standard Maude translation used by the Norton Critical Edition (1966).

5. College Teaching and Culture Wars or: What Really Happened at Duke

1. The group's founding members were Jane Tompkins, Alice Kaplan, and me. Over the ten years of our existence, we added Cathy Davidson and Jan Radway and completed, among other things, a series of memoirs.

2. David Yaffe, "The Department That Fell to Earth: The Deflation of Duke English," *Lingua Franca* 9, no. 1 (1999): 24–31.

3. *Lingua Franca* used this phrase, which was accurate.

4. Though he was tenured at Duke, Goldberg continued to interview job candidates for Johns Hopkins, his previous university, some of them also candidates at Duke. The dual allegiance became a real source of friction.

5. The details here are too ugly to put in the text, hence this footnote. When it became apparent that the external review had gone sideways, I made an appointment with my dean to resign as chair and offer a path forward. The dean told me that he had already released a statement to the press forming a committee that would govern the department along with me and that the statement would appear whether or not I resigned. Given that I had no way to save face or avoid professional damage, I stayed on and ended up leading the committee amiably through the rest of my term. When I asked the dean why he had released to the press information that would ultimately damage not just me but the department and university, he said that he wanted the situation resolved by graduation and was afraid that, if he spoke to me first, I would change his mind.

6. For those interested in minor academic history, Stanley Fish left his position

as chair after the first of these petitions, and a cautious dean did not appoint me as chair at that point even though, as he informed me by phone, the department had nominated me "in a landslide." Once again, this is too much academic trivia to include in the text, but it designates another pivot that might have avoided the meltdown that occurred four years later.

7. *Between Men* (1985; New York: Columbia University Press, 1995); *The Epistemology of the Closet* (1990; Berkeley: University of California Press, 2008); *Tendencies* (Durham, NC: Duke University Press, 1993); *A Dialogue on Love*, pbk. ed. (1999; New York: Penguin Random House, 2000).

8. Koestenbaum's dissertation book was *Double Talk: The Erotics of Male Literary Collaboration* (New York: Routledge, 1989), followed by *The Queen's Throat: Opera, Homosexuality, and the Mystery of Desire* (New York: Picador, 1993). He then wrote public-facing books about Andy Warhol and Jackie Kennedy, memoir, and poetry. Koestenbaum now paints and posts videos that are also performance art to his Instagram account.

9. Jacob Tobia's *Sissy: A Coming of Gender Story* was published by Random House in 2019; Andrea Long Chu's *Females: A Concern* by Verso in 2019.

10. In *Touching Feeling: Affect, Pedagogy, and Performativity* (Durham, NC: Duke University Press, 2002). Sedgwick taught a series of miniseminars at Duke after leaving at which she presented some of these materials.

11. "How to Bring Your Kids up Gay," *Social Text* 29 (1991): 18–27.

12. "A Poem Is Being Written," *Representations* 17 (Winter 1987): 110–43; *A Dialogue on Love* (New York: Beacon, 2000).

13. Edwiga Giunta, introduction to Louise DeSalvo, *Vertigo: A Memoir* (1996; New York: Feminist Press, 2002).

14. See "The Paglia Principle," in my *Crossing Ocean Parkway* (Chicago: University of Chicago Press, 1993).

15. Giunta, introduction to De Salvo, *Vertigo*.

16. In addition to *Vertigo*, the books by Louise DeSalvo mentioned in this paragraph are: *Writing as a Way of Healing: How Telling Our Stories Transforms Our Lives* (New York: HarperSanFrancisco, 1999), *Crazy in the Kitchen: Food, Feuds, and Forgiveness in an Italian American Family* (London: Bloomsbury, 2005), *On Moving: A Writer's Meditation on New Houses, Old Haunts, and Finding Home Again* (London: Bloomsbury, 2009).

17. University of Rhode Island website.

18. Interview with Mary Cappello, https://www.assayjournal.com/mary-cappello .html.

19. Mary Cappello, *Night Bloom: A Memoir* (New York: Beacon, 1998); Mary Cappello, *Life Breaks: A Mood Almanack* (Chicago: University of Chicago Press, 2016).

20. Maria Laurino, *Old World Daughter, New World Mother: An Education in Love and Freedom* (New York: Norton: 2009), 13.

21. Cappello, *Night Bloom*, 73, 186–87.

22. Consider the following, from Maria Laurino, *Old World Daughter*: "As part of the New York media, I had to separate myself from the image of Bensonhurst to be taken seriously" (154). Being harsher than I remembered being, I gave Laurino's *The Italian Americans* a mixed review in the *Italian American Review* 17, no. 1 (1999): 89–93. Like the PBS series that it accompanies, the book's view of Italian-Americans has real flaws, among them conflating Italians and those who immigrated to America in ways that do not work.

23. As is not uncommon in new or ethnic fields, not everyone likes the name Latinx, with some preferring Latino/a or Hispanic. One of several articles on the use of Latinx: Jose A. Del Real, "'Latinx' Hasn't Even Caught on among Latinos. It Never Will," *Washington Post*, December 18, 2020, https://www.washingtonpost.com /outlook/latinx-latinos-unpopular-gender-term/2020/12/18/bf177c5c-3b41-11eb-9276 -ae0ca72729be_story.html. East Coast schools have tended to emphasize Puerto Rican and Caribbean Latinx studies; West Coast schools, Chicano/a and Indigenous studies, as well as Asian-American—often nuancing that field by countries of origin (Chinese, Korean, Thai, Filipino, and so forth), as it well deserves.

24. For example, Edgar Garcia's book of poetry *Skins of Columbus: A Dream Ethnography* (Albany, NY: Fence, 2019) is based on Columbus's diaries during his second voyage along the coast of Central America; Garcia read the diaries at night for four months and wrote poetry each morning. He also writes about the role of *loteria* cards in risk analysis during migration in "A Migrant's *Loteria*: Risk, Fortune, Fate, and Probability in the Borderlands of Juan Felipe Herrera and Artemio Rodriguez's *Loteria Cards and Fortune Poems*," *Modern Philology* 118, no. 3 (2020): 252–76.

6. Elephants: A Meditation on Morality

1. Shana Alexander, *The Astonishing Elephant* (New York: Random House, 2000). The factual information on elephants comes from this source.

2. I write about female primatologists in *Primitive Passions* (New York: Knopf, 1996), chap. 4. Today, many people would say that elephants, like apes, not to mention dogs and cats, are beings analogous to, or even *valuable like*, human beings—for some pet owners all the way to *like children*.

3. The psychologist Jeffrey Moussaieff Masson, who, like me, has written on "the oceanic," makes the case that elephants have emotions in *When Elephants Weep: The Emotional Lives of Animals* (New York: Random House, 2009).

4. Loss of mothers appears in other animal stories as well: for example, Bambi's doe of a mother, a movie trauma experienced by many a child.

5. Jean de Brunhoff, *The Story of Babar: The Little Elephant* (Gipsy, 2016), though there are, of course, other editions, as noted.

6. In *Beyond the Pleasure Principle* (1920), Freud speculated that children toss toys from cribs for this reason, and to bring their mothers back.

7. "What happens when we die?" my older daughter asked after seeing the movie

of *Charlotte's Web*. When I offered her the choice of people's beliefs—a heaven and a hell, or nothing and asked what she thought, she thought a moment and said, "Nothing." We were planting flowers, and I kind of wish I'd qualified that "nothing."

8. Wayne Hepburn, cited in Eric Scigliano, *Love, War, and Circuses: The Age Old Relationship between Elephants and Humans* (New York: Houghton-Mifflin, 2002), 6.

9. Elephants have been endangered for centuries, but the facts become increasingly acute. See a 2019 website about World Elephant Day: https://worldelephantday.org/about/elephants.

10. John Russell, qtd. in Nicholas Fox Weber, *The Art of Babar: The Work of Jean and Laurent de Brunhoff* (New York: Abrams, 1989), 38. Weber adds the reference to Proust.

11. Ann Meinzen Hildebrand, *Jean and Laurent de Brunhoff: The Legacy of Babar* (New York: Twayne, 1991), chronology, vv–xvii. On Jean's sources, see Weber, *The Art of Babar*, 95. The Old Lady in the books wears Cecile's trademark pulled-back hairdo, perhaps as tribute to the mother in the family.

12. Hildebrand gives the general outlines of this story but Weber, *The Art of Babar*, 23, is more complete.

13. The precise number depends on whether we count work he finished for his father or repackaged in slightly different formats.

14. Once he restarted the Babar series, Laurent wrote steadily until 1959, and his books mix and match the primitive: kangaroos from Australia living in Africa—that kind of thing. But in his books, decolonization, like World War II, doesn't matter much either.

15. What's been called the "philosophically crucial dream sequence" was deleted. In it, demon-monsters represent the deadly sins to the left, and light and bright elephant guardian angels dispel them from the right in *Babar the King*. Hildebrand, *Jean and Laurent de Brunhoff*, 9, 41. The same book identifies Cornelius (the aged elephant) with Sanskrit origins. Weber, *The Art of Babar*, reproduces the image in double-page format.

16. The other two ayurvedic types are *vatta* (movement, restlessness) and *pitta* (magnetism, sexuality). Most people have a blend of all three types, with roughly one-third of humans predominantly *kapha*.

17. E. M. Gombrich and Maurice Sendak both praise the drawings' economical renderings. Hildebrand, *Jean and Laurent de Brunhoff*, 27; Weber, *The Art of Babar*, 22.

18. I visit some of this territory in "Reading Dr. Dolittle," in *Crossing Ocean Parkway* (Chicago: University of Chicago Press, 1993).

19. Portions of the Dolittle books and certain parts of Babar seem offensive by modern standards. *Babar's Picnic* (1949) went quietly out of print in the 1960s when Toni Morrison, then an editor at Random House, objected to racism in the book. Gentlemanly and embarrassed, Laurent pulled it.

20. Charles Dickens, "Preliminary Word" to his periodical *Household Words*.

21. There are many sources on Hindu mythology, some more basic than others. This quotation is from Donald Johnson and Jean Johnson, *God and Gods in Hinduism* (New Delhi: Arnold-Heinemann, 1972), 73. See also a more detailed source: W. J. Wilkins, *Hindu Mythology: Vedic and Puranic*, 2nd ed. (1882; Calcutta: Rupa and Co., 1992), 323–34. Wilkins provides a full range of variants in the Ganesh origins myth, which are substantial; while his book is older, it is a good source for variants.

22. Originally, Ganesh's forehead or palms were often adorned by a swastika, a sign of fertility, balance, and harmony—hard for us to read today, after the Nazi misappropriation of the symbol. Modern statues generally omit the sign.

23. Sarah McDonald, *Holy Cow* (New York: Bantam, 2002); Geoff Dyer, *Jeff in Venice / Death in Varanasi* (New York: Vintage, 2009).

24. It's no secret that religious myths and rituals echo around the globe, a veritable structuralist's dream. This myth of the sacrificial god is one of them.

25. I cite classic sources on the oceanic in *Primitive Passions*, 223.

7. Food as Anthropological Lens

1. The bibliography for food studies is quite large but mostly dates from the twenty-first century, when practices of everyday life became routinely studied. Some texts: Bob Ashley, ed., *Food and Cultural Studies* (New York: Routledge, 2004); Jeffrey P. Miller and Jonathan Deutsch, eds., *Food Studies: An Introduction to Research Methods* (New York: Oxford, 2009); Ken Albala, ed., *Routledge International Handbook of Food Studies* (New York: Routledge, 2013).

2. Frequently reprinted, the text I consulted comes from Octagon (New York, 1979).

3. Louise DeSalvo, *Crazy in the Kitchen: Food, Feuds, and Forgiveness in an Italian American Family* (London: Bloomsbury, 2005), 38.

4. I qualify the remark because northern Italy often prefers risotto dishes to red sauce, which is most iconic in the southern half of the country and in cities like Bologna.

The Stark but Familiar Allure of Empty Cities: An Epilogue

1. Both films reflect nuclear anxiety. *The World, the Flesh, and the Devil* (dir. Ranald MacDougall), starring the singer, actor, and activist Harry Belafonte, has a strong racial plot and was suppressed for decades. *On the Beach* (dir. Stanley Kramer) is based on a novel by Neville Shute that was a 1950s bestseller.

2. Starring Will Smith (dir. MacDonald, 2007), *I Am Legend* also has a strong racial subplot, ultimately asserting the need for cooperation across races and even species.

3. Emily St. John Mandel, *Station Eleven: A Novel* (New York: Knopf, 2014); Steven Wright, *The End of October* (New York: Penguin, 2020).

4. Alan Weisman, *The World without Us* (New York: St. Martin's, 2007). The History Channel series was created by David de Vries and aired in 2008–2009.

5. A review of the video game, which the present author admits to not having played, appeared in the *Guardian*. Steve Boxer, "*Tokyo Jungle*—Review," *Guardian*, September 18, 2012, https://www.theguardian.com/technology/gamesblog/2012/sep/18/tokyo-jungle-game-review-ps3.

6. See Brendan I. Koerner, "A Novelist Scours the Honduran Jungle for Pre-Columbian Ruins. The Jungle Scours Him Back," *New York Times*, January 18, 2017, https://www.nytimes.com/2017/01/18/books/review/lost-city-of-monkey-god-douglas-preston.html; and the book's more extended narration: Douglas Preston, *The Lost City of the Monkey God: A True Story* (New York: Grand Central, 2017).

7. Richard Powers, *The Overstory: A Novel* (New York: Norton, 2018); Eduardo Kohn, *How Forests Think: Towards an Anthropology beyond Human* (Berkeley: University of California Press, 2013); Peter Wohlleben, *The Hidden Life of Trees: What They Feel, How They Communicate—Discoveries from a Secret World* (New York: Allen Lane, 2015); and Robert MacFarlane, *Underland: A Deep Time Journey* (New York: Norton, 2019).

8. Roy Scranton, *Learning to Die in the Anthropocene: Reflections on the End of Civilization* (San Francisco: City Lights, 2015); David Wallace-Wells, *The Uninhabitable Earth: Life after Warming* (New York: Tom Duggan, 2019); Bill McKibben, "130 Degrees," *New York Review of Books* 67, no. 14 (2020), https://www.nybooks.com/articles/2020/08/20/climate-emergency-130-degrees/.

Index

9/11, x–xi

Achilles (fictional character), 14–15, 117n9
Aegisthus, 20, 118n9
Aeschylus, 14–16, 26, 118n9, 118n20
affinities, 62–65, 121n8, 121n10
African Americans, 68–69
Agamemnon (fictional character), 14–15, 49
Alan, 107–8
Alexander, Shana, 73
Allen, Woody, 105–6
All Things Shining (Dreyfus and Kelly), 116n6
Alpert, Richard (Baba Ram Dass), 35
American Southwest, 111
animals, 71–72, 110, 122n4. *See also* elephants
Arendt, Hannah, 117n7
Aristotle, 27, 75, 117n8
Arnold, Matthew, 59
associate chair, 58, 60–63, 120n6
Athena, 16, 49
Atonement (McEwan), 27–28, 33
Atreus, 118n9
Atwood, Margaret, 49, 120n6
Austerlitz (Sebald), 28, 119n2
ayurvedic types, 123n16

Babar (fictional character), 72, 75, 123n17; de Brunhoff, C., on, 76–77, 123nn11–12; de Brunhoff, J., on, 76–77, 123nn10–13; de Brunhoff, L., on, 77–78, 123nn13–14, 123n19; Dr. Dolittle compared to, 79,

123n16, 123n19; Random House and, 78–79, 123n15
Baba Ram Dass. *See* Alpert, Richard
Baker, Josephine, 77
Barthes, Roland, 5, 7
Bataille, Georges, ix–x
Becky, xi
Beha, Christopher, 8
Belafonte, Harry, 124n1
"la bella figura" (looking good to others), 1, 103
Benjamin, Walter, 9, 116n9, 117n7
Bensonhurst, 1–3, 68
bhastrika ("skull shining" breath), 38
blissful state (*samadhi*), 35, 107
brain damage, 28–29
breast cancer, 63, 118n13
brother. *See* De Marco, Salvatore, Jr.
brothers and sisters, 16–19, 117nn12–13, 118n15
Brunhoff, Cecile de, 76–77, 123nn11–12
Brunhoff, Jean de, 76–77, 123nn10–13
Brunhoff, Laurent de, 77–78, 123nn13–14, 123n19
Buber, Martin, 118n18
Butler, Samuel, 120nn7–8

Calvino, Italo, 14, 47
cancer deaths, 13, 117nn1–3. *See also specific types*
Cancer World, 17, 117n12
Cappello, Mary, 67
Charlotte's Web (film), 122n7

A professor at Duke University, MARIANNA DE MARCO TORGOVNICK teaches in Durham, North Carolina, during most spring terms a very popular course called "America Dreams American Movies," also the title of an anthology/textbook she published with Cognella in 2018. She lives the majority of the year in New York, where she directs the Duke in New York Arts and Media Program, which brings fifteen to eighteen Duke students to New York during the fall and summer terms to immerse themselves in the city's culture and to work at a variety of internships. She is the author of many books, including *Gone Primitive: Savage Intellects, Modern Lives* (University of Chicago Press) and *Crossing Ocean Parkway* (University of Chicago Press).